CW00719951

PENGUIN PASSNOTES

Jane Eyre

Anne Holker was born on the Isle of Man and educated at
Girton College, Cambridge. After a period of teaching English
Literature and Language at a private school in London,
she became a freelance writer, publishing many articles and
theatrical reviews. She now lives and works in London.

PENGUIN PASSNOTES

CHARLOTTE BRONTË

Jane Eyre

ANNE HOLKER

ADVISORY EDITOR: STEPHEN COOTE, M.A., PH.D.

PENGUIN BOOKS

Penguin Books Ltd, Harmondsworth, Middlesex, England
Viking Penguin Inc., 40 West 23rd Street, New York, New York 10010, U.S.A.
Penguin Books Australia Ltd, Ringwood, Victoria, Australia
Penguin Books Canada Ltd, 2801 John Street, Markham, Ontario, Canada L3R 1B4
Penguin Books (N.Z.) Ltd, 182–190 Wairau Road, Auckland 10, New Zealand

First published 1983
Reprinted 1985, 1986, 1987

Made and printed in Great Britain by
Richard Clay Ltd, Bungay, Suffolk
Filmset in Monophoto Ehrhardt

*The publishers are grateful to the following Examination Boards for
permission to reproduce questions from examination papers used in
individual titles in the Passnotes series:*

*Associated Examining Board, University of Cambridge Local Examinations
Syndicate, Joint Matriculation Board, University of London School
Examinations Department, Oxford and Cambridge Schools Examination
Board, University of Oxford Delegacy of Local Examinations.*

*The Examination Boards accept no responsibility whatsoever for the
accuracy or method of working in any suggested answers given as models.*

Contents

To the Student   7

Introduction: The Life and Background
of Charlotte Brontë   9

Synopsis of *Jane Eyre*   11

An Account of the Plot   20

Characters   66

Commentary   88

Glossary   97

Examination Questions   106

To the Student

This book is designed to help you with your O-level or C.S.E. English Literature examination. It contains a synopsis of the plot, a glossary of the more unfamiliar words and phrases, and a commentary on some of the issues raised by the text. An account of the writer's life is also included for background.

Page references in parentheses are to the Penguin Classics edition, edited by Q. D. Leavis.

When you use this book remember that it is no more than an aid to your study. It will help you find passages quickly and perhaps give you some ideas for essays. But remember: *This book is not a substitute for reading the text and it is your knowledge and your response that matter*. These are the things the examiners are looking for, and they are also the things that will give you the most pleasure. Show your knowledge and appreciation to the examiner, and show them clearly.

Introduction

THE LIFE AND BACKGROUND OF CHARLOTTE BRONTË (1816–55)

For most novelists the inspiration for their work derives from their own experience. Charlotte Brontë is no exception. We can draw many useful parallels between her life and the events in *Jane Eyre*.

Charlotte was the third daughter of Patrick Brontë, the curate of Haworth, a beautiful if bleak village on the North Yorkshire moors. He was the father of six children, all of whom, along with his wife, were to die before him. The story of the Brontë children: Elizabeth, Maria, Charlotte, Branwell, Emily and Anne is thus a tragic one overshadowed by the spectre of lingering illness, loneliness and premature death.

The countryside around Haworth is wild and beautiful and finds many echoes in the landscapes of *Jane Eyre*. However, the Lowood School of the book also has its equivalent in Charlotte's life. At the age of eight she was sent to Cowan Bridge School where she experienced bad food, bad treatment, cruel and hypocritical religion, all in the same manner as Jane Eyre. Helen Burns, indeed, is modelled after her own sister Maria who died as a result of her treatment there.

Thus Charlotte Brontë's life and art were similar to each other from childhood onwards, and it was from this time that the sisters' interest in art sprang. They and their brother Branwell created a rich world of fantasy which was to help form their imaginations and thus create the tone of the novels of Charlotte, Emily and Anne. We can see something of the power of childhood fantasy in chapter 12 of *Jane Eyre*. Even at school, Charlotte was recognized as a brilliant teller of tales.

Charlotte grew into an attractive woman, determined to see the world. Rather than marry the first man who came her way, she vowed to be independent (much of her determination can be glimpsed in Jane's character) and she went to the Continent to learn languages as a preparation to founding a school. In Brussels she fell deeply in love with her teacher, Professor Heger; once again, much of the passionate love of pupil for teacher is reflected in Jane's obsession with Rochester. This theme is found in others of her novels, too: *The Professor* and *Villette*, for example.

The affair with Heger could never blossom and, in the most unhappy stage of her life – with her sisters ill, her father losing his sight and her brother dissipated and dying – Charlotte was driven to write. It was her lifeline to sanity. In a period of extraordinary creativity during 1846 Charlotte was engaged on *Jane Eyre*, Anne on *Agnes Grey* and Emily on *Wuthering Heights*. By the following year all three were published under the pseudonyms of Currer, Acton and Ellis Bell respectively.

Jane Eyre caused a stir in literary London, but much of the pleasure of fame was offset by family tragedy. Anne was dying, her father had increasingly severe problems with his eyes, Branwell too was dying and he was soon followed to the grave by Emily. All three deaths were caused by tuberculosis.

Through all this, Charlotte continued to write and enhance her reputation. Her friends now included the great novelist Mrs Gaskell who was later to write her biography. Rather surprisingly, after rejecting a number of offers, Charlotte married her father's dull but loving curate in 1854. The marriage was a short-lived happiness. Eight months pregnant, and halfway through her new novel *Emma*, Charlotte too died of tuberculosis on 30 March 1855. She left her husband and father, in Mrs Gaskell's moving words, 'sitting desolate and alone in the old grey house'. She was not quite forty.

Synopsis of Jane Eyre

Jane Eyre can be conveniently divided up into those sections which are marked by Jane's five major journeys. These journeys are from:

1. Gateshead to Lowood in the January of Jane's tenth year (ch. 5).

2. Lowood to Thornfield in the October of Jane's eighteenth year (ch. 11).

3. Thornfield to Gateshead and back the following May (ch. 21).

4. Thornfield to Marsh End the following July (ch. 28).

5. Moor House to Thornfield in the May of the next year (ch. 36).

The first five chapters of *Jane Eyre* describe Jane's life with the Reeds at Gateshead Hall. We plunge straight into the narrative: Jane is taunted by the repulsive John Reed and is unjustly blamed for the argument, and sent to the dreaded 'red-room' where Mr Reed died (p. 44). While the terrified Jane huddles in the red-room, she considers her life at Gateshead. She is an orphan, and her Aunt Reed barely tolerates her presence in the house. Her three cousins, Eliza, John and Georgiana are spoiled and cruel, yet are never reprimanded. As Jane broods on the injustice of this she becomes more and more frightened at being alone in a supposedly haunted room. She begs Mrs Reed to release her, but the stern woman is intransigent. Eventually Jane faints with terror, and when she regains consciousness sees a physician staring worriedly at her (p. 51). Mr Lloyd recognizes the signs of mental stress and tries to question Jane about her life. Jane will only admit that she is miserable and, after further questioning, that she would like to escape from the house and attend school. Mrs Reed makes arrangements for her niece to be sent to a school, and invites Mr Brocklehurst to Gateshead to interview Jane (p. 63). Mr Brocklehurst, we learn, administers a charity boarding-school called Lowood. Mrs Reed, in front of Mr Brockle-hurst, accuses Jane of deceit and he avers that the child must indeed have a 'wicked heart'. Jane is furious that her character be so spitefully blackened, and after Brocklehurst has left, rounds on her aunt, accusing her of cruelty and hypocrisy (p. 68). Mrs Reed is visibly shaken: so much so that Jane's 'triumph' becomes soured. However, plans for the girl's removal to school proceed, and at the beginning of chapter 5 we see Jane setting off on her journey to Lowood.

On her first night at Lowood, Jane is too tired to assimilate her surroundings. Next day, however, she experiences the bitter cold of the place, and the paltry and disgusting food. In the afternoon, Jane meets Helen Burns, who describes some of the teachers to the new girl (p. 81). Later, Jane witnesses Helen being punished by Miss Scatcherd. Jane questions Helen more closely and Helen shares with Jane her Christian philosophy of 'turning the other cheek'. Jane feels she is incapable of forgiving Mrs Reed in the way Helen forgives the tyrannical teacher (p. 88).

After a few weeks at Lowood, Jane is confronted by Mr Brocklehurst. Jane is made a public mockery by Brocklehurst who orders her to stand on a stool amidst the other pupils as punishment for her deceitful ways (p. 98). Jane bears this well, but afterwards she is found weeping by Helen Burns. Miss Temple takes both girls into her study and cheers Jane considerably by promising to write to Mr Lloyd, the doctor, for corroboration of Jane's story. Jane is impressed by the intellectual relationship that the two women have, and is also worried by Miss Temple's apparent despair at Helen's health (p. 103).

Months pass. It is now May, and although the countryside around Lowood is serene and beautiful, typhus fever has caught hold of the school, and at least half the pupils are affected. Jane learns that Helen's sickness is not typhus, but tuberculosis. One evening, Jane visits Helen and finds the young woman on her death bed. To comfort her, Jane slips into her bed. Next morning she finds that Helen has died (p. 114).

The narrative now jumps eight years. We learn that there has been a public outcry against the terrible conditions at Lowood and, after Mr Brocklehurst's power has diminished, the school becomes a far healthier, happier place. Miss Temple is engaged to be married and, feeling that with the departure of this much-loved principal, Lowood will not be the same, Jane places an advertisement in the local paper for a position as governess (p. 119). In due course Jane receives a reply from a Mrs Fairfax of Thornfield Hall, whose charge is a little girl of under ten. As she is about to leave for Thornfield, Jane receives a surprise visitor: Bessie, the only soul who had shown her any kindness during her stay at Gateshead (p. 122). Bessie brings Jane up to date on the Reed family, and the news is not cheering: the sisters hate one another, and John has turned to a life of dissipation. Bessie mentions that seven years ago, Jane's uncle John Eyre had called on the Reeds, hoping to meet his niece. They speculate a little on the sort of man Mr Eyre might be, and then Bessie leaves for Gateshead, and Jane sets off for Thornfield (p. 125).

After a day's journey, Jane arrives at Thornfield and is greeted by Mrs Fairfax, whom Jane takes to be the lady of the house (p. 127). Next day Mrs Fairfax explains that she is simply the housekeeper and that the house is owned by a Mr Rochester whose ward, Miss Varens, Jane has been hired to teach. In due course, Jane meets Adèle Varens and her French maid (p. 132). She also learns a little about Mr Rochester and is shown round the imposing Hall. While gazing from the upper storey at the view below, Jane hears a horrible, demonic laugh (p. 138). Mrs Fairfax explains that it comes from Grace Poole's room. Grace is introduced. She is a housemaid, and to Jane looks far too homely to possess such a tragic laugh. Three months pass, and Jane is content if rather bored at Thornfield. One evening she takes a long walk to break the monotony. She is aware of a horse bearing down upon her, and is frightened lest it be the legendary 'Gytrash'. The horse is mounted, however, for Jane hears swearing and cursing as its rider takes a fall (p. 144). She attempts to help the rather fearsome looking rider back onto his horse, explaining that she is the new governess at Thornfield Hall. When Jane returns to the house, she recognizes the dog basking by the fire in the hall. It is the same dog that accompanied the injured rider. Jane learns that Mr Rochester is making one of his infrequent visits to Thornfield Hall. Next evening, Jane meets her master in his study (p. 151). He questions her closely about her time at Lowood, and her talents. Jane shows him some of her drawings and he appears much interested. Later, Mrs Fairfax explains to Jane that Rochester has had an unhappy life, but she does not elaborate save to say that he has broken with his family. A few days later Jane has another interview with Rochester and learns more of his character (p. 162). He asks whether she thinks him handsome, and somewhat taken aback she admits that she does not. Rochester then intimates that although fortune has been unkind to him, he knows he has it within him to be a better person. At Jane's age, he adds, he had been unsullied by the world. Jane barely understands Rochester's philosophizing, but, as he admits, she is a sympathetic listener.

On a subsequent occasion, Rochester expands on his theme, describing his dissipated life on the Continent when he was younger (p. 172). He also explains that Adèle is the daughter of a former mistress, Céline, who tricked him so unkindly that he fell out of love with her. Rather than be shocked, Jane insists that this knowledge will make her even more kindly disposed to Adèle. Jane also finds herself drawn more closely to Rochester, for she believes that, for all his appearances, he has an excellent character underneath. That night, Jane is awakened by Grace Poole's demonic laugh. As she rushes out to find Mrs Fairfax, she sees smoke billowing from Rochester's room and, without a moment's hesitation, douses the flames and rescues her sleeping master (p. 174). Next morning she views Grace with suspicion and dislike. However, the strange servant simply advises Jane to keep her bedroom door locked in future, and shows no apparent signs of guilt. Rochester has, without a word to Jane, left Thornfield to stay with the Eshton family ten miles away. There, Mrs Fairfax explains, Blanche Ingram is also staying, and the housekeeper hints that there may well be a match between the beautiful Blanche and the master of Thornfield. Shaken by this news, and by the suspicion that she has become infatuated with Rochester, Jane forces herself to paint two portraits: one of herself, a plain governess, and one as she imagines the ravishing Blanche to look like (p. 190). She is soon to meet her 'rival'. The house-party arrives at

Thornfield, and Blanche is as beautiful as Jane had imagined. She is also, on closer acquaintance, unpleasantly haughty, and Jane doubts whether Rochester can possibly find her charming. Jane has plenty of opportunity to observe the 'lovers', as she is invited into the drawing-room every evening. It is while watching a game of charades that Jane realizes that she has fallen deeply and irrevocably in love with Rochester (p. 203).

One day, two strangers arrive at Thornfield: a friend of Rochester's from the West Indies called Mason, and an old gypsy woman who wants to tell the fortunes of the young single women in the party (p. 221). Blanche is keen to have her fortune told, but emerges from her 'consultation' looking very sour indeed. Jane then visits the gypsy herself, and discovers 'she' is none other than Mr Rochester in disguise (p. 231). Jane gives very little away, but learns that Rochester indeed plans to marry Blanche. She informs him of Mason's arrival and is astounded to see her master quail. Later that night, Jane is awakened by a terrible shrieking. Rochester assures his guest that it is only a servant having a nightmare, but when everyone has disappeared, he asks Jane for her help. Mason is in one of the third-storey rooms, near where Grace Poole's demonic laughter is sometimes heard, and he has obviously been attacked: both stabbed and bitten. While Rochester fetches a doctor, Jane tends the injured man, turning over in her mind the deepening mystery of Thornfield Hall. Rochester does not enlighten her further, although he leaves her in no doubt that Grace has been the perpetrator of the attack. He admits that he hates Thornfield and fears what it symbolizes for him.

Chapter 21 serves to lessen the tension of the novel. Jane has a visit from Bessie who brings her grim tidings of Gateshead. Mrs Reed is dying, having had a stroke following the suicide of her son. Apparently she has expressed a wish to see Jane once more, and so, no longer harbouring any grudges against the woman, Jane asks permission of Rochester to attend her death bed.

Jane arrives at Gateshead in May (p. 255). Mrs Reed is indeed very sick, and on Jane's first visit appears to be just as hardened against her as she had been years ago. However, a week later, Jane speaks to the dying woman again, and learns the truth behind her animosity. Apparently, Jane's mother had been Mr Reed's favourite sister, and so when she died in penury, Reed had taken in her baby daughter. Mrs Reed had been very jealous of the baby, and maddened when her husband made her promise on his death bed to look after Jane as if she were one of her own children. Mrs Reed's other revelation is that three years previously John Eyre, Jane's uncle in Madeira, had written to her advising her that he intended to make Jane his beneficiary on his death. Mrs Reed had told him that Jane had in fact died, struck down with typhus at Lowood (p. 266).

After Mrs Reed's death, Jane gets to know the Reed daughters rather better. Eliza reveals her plans to become a nun in France, and Georgiana shares with Jane her frustrations at being cooped up in Gateshead. (At this point Jane tells her readers that Eliza's ambitions were realized, that she became in time Mother Superior, while her sister married an eligible if 'worn out' man of fashion.)

When Jane arrives back at Thornfield, her happiness at returning to the house and to Rochester is made poignant by the awareness that when Rochester marries both she and Adèle will have to leave. The happy family atmosphere will be shattered. Jane confides this to Rochester when, later, they are in the garden together (p. 278). She makes it clear that she loves him, and that parting will be very painful for her. At this Rochester admits that it is she whom he wishes to marry, not Blanche at all, and that he loves her passionately (p. 282). Jane agrees to become Mrs Edward Rochester. However, preparations for their wedding are not as happy as the reader might wish. Mrs Fairfax offers Jane dire warnings about Mr Rochester's integrity, and Jane begins to fear that she will lose her independence by marrying someone so much richer than herself. As a result, she writes to her uncle in Madeira, alerting him to her existence. But by far the most macabre event to overshadow Jane's happiness takes place two nights before the wedding. Jane has terrifying dreams in which Thornfield appears as a ruin. When she wakes, she sees a strange, appalling looking woman in her room. This apparition proceeds to tear her wedding veil in two (p. 311). The next morning, Jane is half convinced that her 'visitor' had been another dream, yet, to her horror, she finds the veil has indeed been torn in two. Rochester is alarmed when Jane tells him about her frightening experiences, and arranges that she spend her last night before the wedding in Adèle's nursery, the door firmly bolted.

On the morning of their wedding, it is clear that Rochester is in a great hurry to get the service over, and has arranged that he and his bride leave directly for their honeymoon. The service is dramatically interrupted by Briggs, a solicitor, and Mason, who claim to have proof of Rochester's bigamy (p. 317). Rochester admits the truth of this, and invites Briggs, the vicar, Mason (who it appears, is Rochester's brother-in-law) and Jane to meet his wife. Everything now fits together: Grace Poole is the mad Mrs Rochester's keeper; the lunatic is the same 'apparition' which had visited Jane two nights previously. Later, Rochester tries to explain to Jane the circumstances of his marriage. She hears him out, and is indeed moved to pity by the way he had been tricked and abused. However, she cannot consent to becoming his mistress, however much she loves him. Next morning she leaves Thornfield, heartbroken and distressed, knowing only that she must remove herself from temptation (p. 347). She hails a passing carriage and asks to be taken as far as her money will allow. Two days later, Jane alights at a crossroads. Exhausted, she passes the night sleeping on the bare moorland. Next day she tries to find employment in the nearby village of Morton. However, there appears to be no work, and no one takes pity on her. As yet, she cannot quite bring herself to beg, but next day, after a terrible night sleeping on the open moor again, she becomes bolder and more desperate. As evening approaches, her reserves of hope and strength are all but wasted. She makes her way to a cottage and peers in at the domestic scene (p. 357). When she begs for bread, however, the housekeeper turns her away, and Jane sinks to the ground, thinking her end has come.

A young man finds her at the door and brings her inside (p. 362). He is the brother of the two girls Jane has seen through the window and between them they revive Jane. When she is fully recovered, Jane learns that St John is a local parson, and his two sisters Diana and Mary are governesses. Their father has recently died, and because their father had quarrelled with his rich brother they have no expectation of wealth. Jane does not reveal much about her own life, and certainly does not explain why she had to leave Thornfield in such haste. St John promises to find her employment and after some time asks Jane whether she would like to run a charity school for girls in his parish. When the time comes for Diana and Mary to return to their posts, Jane and St John move to the village of Morton: St John to live in the parsonage, Jane to live in the schoolhouse cottage. Her life as schoolmistress is uneventful, yet quite satisfying, even though she is still haunted by dreams of Rochester, and she longs for his love. She gets to know the beautiful and rich heiress, Rosamond Oliver, whose money finances the little school (p. 381). It is clear that this woman adores St John and that he is moved by her beauty. However, as he explains to Jane, he cannot risk indulging in earthly pleasures. Much as he is tempted to succumb to Rosamond, his vocation as a parson, and then, hopefully, as a missionary, is too important.

One snowy November evening, St John visits Jane in her cottage and acquaints her with some startling news (p. 403). Her uncle in Madeira has died leaving her twenty thousand pounds. Jane is more thrilled by the second piece of news, which is that her mysterious uncle is the rich brother of St John's father. She has suddenly acquired three cousins. She also learns that Rochester has been trying frantically to find her, and she begs St John for any news of her old master. He can tell her very little, however, and Jane fears he may have left England to resume his dissipated life on the Continent. Jane persuades St John to agree to her plan of dividing her new-found fortune between her three cousins, so that St John may marry Rosamond, and Diana and Mary give up their jobs as governesses.

Christmas approaches and Jane refurbishes Moor House, the parsonage, in preparation for a happy family gathering. Diana and Mary are overjoyed at the house's transformation, but St John thinks Jane is wasting her valuable time with domestic chores, and puts rather a 'damper' on the Christmas spirit.

In the months that follow the cousins lead a harmonious life together, each pursuing their own study. St John is learning Hindustani in preparation for his mission to India. He asks Jane to learn it with him, and so she relinquishes her German studies. One day,

Jane is particularly troubled by recurring thoughts of Rochester (she has had no replies to letters sent to Thornfield), she is also worn down by the discipline of learning Hindustani. St John takes her on a bracing walk across the moorland, and then makes an extraordinary proposition: that Jane accompany him to India as a fellow helpmate and wife (p. 426). Jane replies that she will go to India with him, gladly, but not as his wife. They do not love one another she explains, and such a 'marriage of convenience' would be abhorrent to her. St John is adamant. It would be morally wrong, he believes, for Jane to be with him in any role other than that of wife. They part on bad terms, although St John seems confident that Jane will change her mind. This almost happens when days later St John tries to persuade her and Jane feels the strength of his will swamping her indecision. Just as she is about to relent, however, she 'hears' Rochester's voice calling to her (p. 444). Her mind is at once made up. Her duty and her love belong to Rochester, and next morning she sets out for Thornfield.

A terrible shock awaits her. Thornfield is a blackened ruin, just as her dream had foreseen. Horrified, she returns to Millcote and asks the host at the inn for news of Rochester (p. 450). It transpires that Mrs Rochester started the fire in one of her mad fits, and in his attempt to rescue her, Rochester had a terrible fall, resulting in his becoming blind. Mrs Rochester herself has died. On hearing that Rochester has now moved to Ferndean, a manor house some thirty miles away, Jane orders a carriage to take her there. Rochester is in the care of his servants, John and Mary, and is indeed blind and clearly broken-hearted. His joy at Jane's arrival is touching; he can hardly believe that his prayers have been answered (p. 458). He asks Jane to marry him for the second time, and for the second time she accepts (p. 469).

The narrative now jumps ten years. Jane and Rochester are still blissfully happy, and to crown their happiness Rochester's sight has been partially recovered. Diana and Mary have also married, but not St John, whose missionary work has brought him, at last, the peace and fulfilment he had so long sought.

An Account of the Plot

Charlotte Brontë tells her heroine's story in a direct and simple way. She describes each important event that happens to Jane in the order in which it occurred. This is called a chronological narrative. She adds suspense and drama by keeping from both Jane and the reader important details about other characters and their background. The most obvious example of this is Mr Rochester's marriage. The same is also true of Jane's relationship to St John Rivers. By telling the story in a straightforward manner, Charlotte Brontë can concentrate on the way in which Jane develops from a little girl to a mature and married woman.

CHAPTER 1, *pp. 39–43*

Jane Eyre is a ten-year-old orphan living in the house of her aunt, Mrs Reed. Mrs Reed had reluctantly taken Jane in after the death of her parents who were poor and had married for love (p. 58). Mrs Reed is herself a widow and she has three children: Eliza, John and Georgiana, whom Jane regards as physically more attractive than herself. All three Reed children, particularly John, are spoiled and unkind. They delight in being cruel to Jane, and it is as their victim that we first see her. She has been excluded from the family group for her supposed bad behaviour. In a forthright way she asks how she has misbehaved but is given no adequate answer. We then see the lonely little girl slip into the breakfast room to console herself with a book. Safe behind the curtains, she is finally interrupted by John. John is a weak bully who can inspire 'terror' in Jane. He is never told off for this by either the servants or his mother. John hits Jane, supposedly for being rude to his mother and because she likes to be on her own. He then asks for the book she has been reading and says it is his. He throws the book at her and she cuts her head on the door as she moves to avoid it. The bleeding Jane speaks sharply to John and he rushes at her. The two girls go to fetch Mrs Reed who orders the servants to lock Jane in the red-room as a punishment.

CHAPTER 2, *pp. 44–50*

Jane is taken struggling to the red-room where she is threatened with being tied to a chair and is firmly told yet again that she is living off Mrs Reed's charity and so should be dutiful and grateful. Jane is then locked on her own in the terrifying room. It was here, nine years before, that Mr Reed died. Frightened and angry, Jane analyses the spite of the Reed children. Looking back on these events as an adult, she realizes that she was disliked because she could not join in with them or feel any affection towards them. She is punished while they get away with their insolence.

It begins to get dark. Jane thinks more and more about death, and the room becomes increasingly a place of terror. Finally the little girl can stand it no longer and she rushes to the door and rattles the lock. This brings the servants running and she begs to be set free (p. 49). Mrs Reed now arrives: she is appalled by the noise and demands that Jane stay in the room until she has learned to be submissive. She can only see Jane as a wicked and lying girl.

CHAPTER 3, *pp. 51–8*

Jane wakes from a fit and finds herself in her own room with the kindly local apothecary. When her own children are ill Mrs Reed sends for a proper physician, but for Jane this less qualified but kindly man is good enough. The servants believe that Jane has seen a ghost.

So terrible have these events been that they have had a permanent effect on Jane's nerves. She forgives Mrs Reed, however, because she realizes that the woman was trying to do the best for her as she saw it (p. 52).

Jane is in low spirits for some while. She cannot eat properly and even her favourite books no longer interest her. Bessie, one of the kinder servants, tries to comfort her, but when she is finally left alone with the apothecary she tells him the truth about her state. His reactions to her story are not obvious, but clearly he is shocked. He gently questions her, discovers that she appears to have no relations, and then asks her if she would like to go to school (p. 57). She says that she would and the apothecary mentions this to Mrs Reed. It is decided that Jane should indeed be sent away to school. She hears this from the gossip of the servants, learning at the same time the sad story of her parents (p. 58).

CHAPTER 4, *pp. 59–72*

Jane gathers her strength for the promised change. Mrs Reed has told her children to ignore her in the meantime and the spirited Jane retorts that they are not fit to associate with her anyway (p. 59). Mrs Reed, not without some justification, is furious and sweeps Jane off to her bedroom. Here Jane tells her that old Mr Reed would never have behaved in this cruel way. Mrs Reed, deeply shocked, smacks her.

Two and a half months pass. Jane spends a wretched Christmas at the house and then, in the middle of January, after a period of all but solitary confinement, she is told she has a visitor and is hurriedly got ready. She is thrust, terrified, into the breakfast-room where she confronts Mr Brocklehurst (p. 63). He is a vast, grim, terrifying man. Despite running a school he has no love for children. He immediately sees Jane as sinful and talks to her about death, Hell and repentance. Jane is seen as yet more wicked when she confesses to disliking the Psalms (p. 65). Jane is about to stand up for herself when Mrs Reed tells Mr Brocklehurst that Jane is disobedient and deceitful. Jane is hurt, knowing that this account of her is likely to spoil any chance she may have of future happiness. Mr Brocklehurst replies that his school is run on Christian lines and that Jane will be disciplined into humility. He describes his school and how it is run (p. 66) and we now have a more complete picture of the hypocritical nature of Mr Brocklehurst's religion.

When Mr Brocklehurst has gone Mrs Reed orders Jane from the room. The girl is about to go when her need to speak out against her terrible treatment gets the better of her. She denies that she is a liar and says that the description better fits Mrs Reed's own children. The excited, high-spirited Jane tells Mrs Reed that she hates her, disowns her and is sickened by her. From her outburst, her passionate defence of herself, Jane derives a great sense of freedom and joy (p. 69). Indeed, so powerful has her speech been that Mrs Reed is silenced and, as the little girl leaves, whispers that she will surely send her to school as soon as she can.

Jane realizes that she has won; she has fought and been the victor in her first struggle for the freedom to be herself. This is crucial to her character. However, Charlotte Brontë shows that she is still a little girl, for her outburst leaves her confused (pp. 69–70). She runs outside and is chased by the servant Bessie to whom she can speak now with much greater self-confidence than before. With this new power she can also be more affectionate. The chapter closes with the important impression of self-confidence won and with it the strength of love. This is an early, crucial stage in Jane's maturing.

CHAPTER 5, *pp. 73–84*

A few days later Jane leaves Gateshead very early for her new school. She has refused a kind parting word to Mrs Reed and she now travels the fifty miles to the school on her own. She is free of Gateshead, her first prison, and arrives in the dark and the rain at her new school.

At first she is confused by the noise and bustle. Charlotte Brontë is also concerned to show the discipline, regimentation and poor food that characterize the school. The exhausted child goes to bed to be woken very early the next day for more than an hour of prayers and Bible readings at the end of which dawn has broken and the girls are led off to eat a revolting breakfast. Jane cannot eat it and cries of protest are heard from the other girls. The dreary lessons then begin.

All is not hopeless, however. We encounter Miss Temple (pp. 79–80), a woman Jane can admire at once. She is the superintendent of the school and she cares for the girls in her charge. She orders a bread and cheese lunch for them to make up for the dreadful breakfast.

In the break, Jane wanders out into the garden where she reads an inscription which informs us that the name of the school is Lowood. Jane also hears a cough and turns round to find her first friend: Helen Burns. The young girl is reading *Rasselas*, a short novel by Dr Johnson in which life is shown to be very painful and that the best way to endure it is through patient faith and hope. The book, of course, is a key to Helen Burns's personality, just as her cough is a clue to the way in which she will die. The girl has tuberculosis.

Jane and Helen talk. Jane learns the names and something of the characters of the teachers and is told that Miss Temple is by far the best; she is both good and clever.

During afternoon school Jane sees Helen Burns humiliatingly punished and is amazed and impressed by the patient way she puts up with it. This is Jane's first sight of Helen Burns's brave philosophy in action. It is called stoicism.

CHAPTER 6, *pp. 85–91*

The girls rise before dawn and find that their washing water has frozen over. Later in the day, as Jane watches Helen Burns's continued humiliation, she sees her being punished for being unwashed. She is cruelly beaten.

The lessons are very dull indeed and consist largely of learning strings of facts by heart. Jane, however, is not as unhappy as might be expected. She explains that because she has come from such a loveless background she cannot feel homesick (p. 87). She questions Helen further that evening and asks her if she wants to leave the school since she is so badly treated there. Helen replies that she does not: she is getting an education and accepts that her punishment is very often justified. Jane is surprised and shows again her independence and tendency to revolt. She is amazed by Helen's stoical philosophy but knows in her heart that it is somehow wrong (p. 88). Both girls are enthusiastic about Miss Temple, but when Helen again unfolds her stoic philosophy Jane is forced to answer back. She finds that her new friend accepts suffering far too passively (p. 90). We glimpse here Jane's independence.

CHAPTER 7, *pp.* 92–9

Jane describes the passing of her first term, a time of coldness, dreariness and occasional moments of joy. She then describes a visit by Mr Brocklehurst to his school. Jane immediately feels that he will threaten what little happiness she can find there. She describes his mean, money-conscious and utterly unimaginative orders about clothes, food and other necessities. He asks about the lunch Miss Temple had ordered for the girls on the first day of Jane's attendance at the school and the full force of his hypocrisy is felt when he declares (p. 95) that such pampering is unChristian and a threat to the well-being of the souls of the girls. When he sees a girl with naturally curling and lovely red hair he considers it a sinful luxury and orders it to be cut off. It is noteworthy that his own two daughters, who enter at this point, are luxuriously dressed. Hypocrisy could not be made clearer.

At last he sees Jane who has dropped her slate behind which she was hiding her face (p. 97). He forgives her, but she is revolted by him and, saying to herself that she is no Helen Burns, she feels her impulse to revolt arise. Jane has tried to hide herself from Mr Brockle-hurst but he now orders that she be placed on a high stool in the middle of the room. With Jane in public view, Brocklehurst proceeds to humiliate her by preaching a sermon on the fault that Mrs Reed has outlined: namely that Jane is a liar. He declares that she is a sick person and to help her cure she is to remain on the chair for half an hour after he has gone. Jane, tormented by her anger, receives strength from watching the patience of the still-suffering Helen.

CHAPTER 8, *pp. 100–106*

During the evening Jane weeps at her humiliation. This seems all the worse because she has just begun to make some real improvement in her work. She is comforted by Helen Burns, but for all the girl can bring her some ease, Jane still feels that Helen's quiet patience is not for her. The girls kiss each other affectionately and are then invited to Miss Temple's room.

This, of course, is a great treat for both girls. Jane explains how humiliated she feels and how all eighty of the girls in the school must despise her. Miss Temple says that this is not necessarily the case and asks Jane to tell her her life story. This Jane does, being careful not to overstate her case (p. 103). Miss Temple replies that she knows Mr Lloyd, the apothecary, and she will write to him and ask if what Jane has told her is true; if it is, then Jane will be publicly cleared. Miss Temple already believes her to be innocent.

The girls are offered tea. The food that arrives is meagre and a request for more is refused. Miss Temple makes up the quantity with seedcake of her own. As they eat they talk. The strength and kindness of Miss Temple brings out the best in the girls. Helen in particular glows in her presence, and as she talks with Miss Temple Jane is amazed by the quality of their conversation (p. 105). We are made to see how positive is the effect of true Christian charity rather than the life-denying faith of Mr Brocklehurst.

We learn later that Mr Lloyd, the apothecary, has confirmed all that Jane told Miss Temple about her life and she is publicly cleared of all blame, as promised. Now, in a climate of love and fairness, she begins to flourish. Her work improves, she begins really to enjoy her art and to love Lowood because of the love she herself has found there (p. 106).

The importance of the positive power of real love is powerfully shown to us.

CHAPTER 9, *pp. 107–14*

Spring comes and Jane rejoices at its loveliness. However, with spring an epidemic of typhus also comes to the school. Jane, who remains healthy, is free to wander as she will. Helen becomes very ill indeed and Jane, who has been enjoying nature and life so much, is appalled to hear that her friend is dying of consumption (p. 111). She is firmly resolved to see her.

Jane makes her way to Miss Temple's room where Helen is dying. Jane is profoundly moved by the sight of her and by the way she calmly and fearlessly faces death (p. 113). After expressing her religious convictions the exhausted Helen falls asleep. Jane too eventually sleeps. When she wakes the following morning she learns that Helen is dead.

CHAPTER 10, *pp. 115–24*

The outbreak of typhus at Lowood school results in an inquiry and Mr Brocklehurst is obliged to surrender most of his duties to a more suitable man.

Charlotte Brontë now jumps eight years in her heroine's autobiography, years in which she learns her lessons, becomes head girl and finally a teacher at the same institution. Miss Temple eventually marries and leaves. Jane finds that much of the pleasure has now gone out of her life and she begins to feel restless. The independent spirit we have noted longs for freedom (p. 117). With great secrecy, Jane advertises for a new position and eventually receives a letter from a Mrs Fairfax offering her the post of private tutor to a little girl of ten. References are sent and she is accepted.

Jane is on the point of leaving the school when she receives a surprise visit from Bessie, the one servant who had shown her any kindness at Mrs Reed's house. She tells Jane news of Mrs Reed's troublesome daughters and then of John who has turned out to be a weak-willed and dissipated young man. Bessie sees that Jane, poor though she still is, has become an educated and refined young lady, her painting being particularly remarkable. Her most important news, however, is of a distant relation of Jane's: a Mr Eyre who lives in Madeira. He, as we shall see later, will be most important to Jane's future.

CHAPTER 11, *pp. 125–39*

Alone and slightly frightened, Jane makes her way to Thornfield Hall, the home of Mr Rochester and the place of her new appointment. When she arrives she meets the charming, elderly Mrs Fairfax who receives her with great kindness. The exhausted Jane offers a prayer of thanks and then goes to bed. In the morning she is able to see something of the scale and luxury of Thornfield and is impressed by it. Jane also learns of the existence of Mr Rochester for the first time (p. 131), and is then told that her pupil is the ward of her absentee landlord. She is introduced to Adèle who has received a strong French upbringing. The little girl is quick-witted and precocious and has clearly been rather spoilt.

After morning lessons, Jane sees more of the house and continues to be impressed. She is surprised that, despite the fact that the master is not in residence, everything is ready for his return. Mrs Fairfax tells her that Mr Rochester is a fastidious man, a great traveller and a master who is likely to turn up without a great deal of warning.

He is clearly an interesting character, but all Mrs Fairfax will tell Jane is that she can never be sure whether he is serious or joking and that he is a good master.

Jane asks if there are any ghosts in the house; she is told that there are not. For a long while she is kept in ignorance of the horror locked away on the third floor: this is Mr Rochester's mad wife. Even when she hears mad laughter that day (p. 138) she suspects nothing. She is told that it is only a servant, Grace Poole, whom she sees and finds to be the least romantic and ghostly person imaginable. The alert reader, of course, is far more suspicious.

CHAPTER 12, *pp. 140–49*

Jane is fairly happy in her new position. She adopts a modern and mature attitude towards her pupil (p. 140). But she has to admit she is bored. In a most important paragraph, Charlotte Brontë has Jane utter her own thoughts about the place and nature of women (p. 141).

Jane continues to hear the laughter of the woman she supposes to be Grace Poole but takes little notice of it.

On a rare day off, Jane goes for a long walk. Evening falls and, alone in the countryside, she suddenly hears a noise. She is startled and for a moment supposes it must be the 'Gytrash', a legendary wild animal that was supposed to haunt the nearby lanes. What she has heard, of course, though she does not know this, is Mr Rochester riding home. Charlotte Brontë has here deliberately associated him with the idea of the supernatural and the sinister. It is a vital clue to the way in which she wants to characterize him.

Mr Rochester's horse has slipped on the ice and he himself has fallen and hurt himself. Jane comes to his aid. It is as a would-be helpmate that she first meets Rochester, and it is in this same role that she will eventually marry him. Now, when she first sees him, she feels at ease with him. This is not because he is conventionally handsome, far from it. She describes him (p. 146) as dark, stern, angry and rather rough. He is also nearly middle-aged.

Without telling her who he is, Rochester questions Jane, discovers that she is the governess at his house and orders her to fetch his wandering horse. She has pleasure in obeying him. He leans heavily on her, remounts his horse and then, asking for his whip, rides off. Jane eventually returns to the rather dreary prospect of an evening at Thornfield. She does not realize that this brief meeting will alter the whole of her life. Slowly she walks through the house until she comes to Mrs Fairfax's room. There she sees a dog similar to the one belonging to the nameless rider of that afternoon. She calls it by the name she heard it given: Pilot. The dog responds to her. From one of the servants Jane learns that, after an accident, the master has come home. Pilot is Mr Rochester's dog.

CHAPTER 13, *pp. 150–59*

Jane feels that life at Thornfield has improved with Mr Rochester's presence. He is someone from another world, a world very different to that Jane has known.

She is required to present Adèle to him at six. Mrs Fairfax gives her a little brooch to brighten her appearance a little. By the light of the candles, Jane recognizes the traveller she has helped, recognizes his strong face and the grim air about him. She also sees that he has a powerful body.

Rochester behaves in a very off-hand manner, but this seems to put Jane at her ease. A sophisticated man with highly polished manners would have troubled her.

Mr Rochester questions Jane about her past. At first he jokes about her being a fairy, but from her sensible and modest answers he begins to derive the impression of a strong, intelligent and above all simple woman. He asks her if she plays the piano. He is unimpressed by her playing, but when she shows him her paintings (p. 157) he clearly approves both of their technical merit and their passionate inspiration. He realizes that this good and simple girl has depths of feeling. When he has seen the pictures, he dismisses her.

Jane confesses to Mrs Fairfax that she finds Mr Rochester rather abrupt (p. 158). Mrs Fairfax agrees but tries to give some background to this by explaining that he has had family troubles (p. 159). He had an older brother who died some nine years before. It was to him that his money-minded father left all his wealth. To make his own fortune Rochester was forced into a 'painful position'. At this point neither Jane nor the reader is told that this 'painful position' was his marriage to the lunatic woman hidden upstairs, of whose existence Jane is still unaware. On the death of his brother, Mr Rochester inherited the whole estate. This wealth has not, however, brought him happiness. Mrs Fairfax comes back to the picture of her restless, travelling master. She does not make clear why Rochester should so avoid Thornfield Hall.

CHAPTER 14, *pp. 160–71*

Chapter 14 shows Jane and Mr Rochester becoming better acquainted. Theirs is far from the talk of conventional young lovers: Rochester remains haughty; Jane, for her part, preserves her independence.

Rochester's presents for Adèle have arrived. The little girl bubbles over with enthusiasm and Rochester summons Mrs Fairfax to entertain her. He can now talk to Jane. His sternness continues to impress her (p. 162) but his behaviour is so blunt that she wonders if he is drunk. Rochester tells her that he has been almost wholly hardened by the world (p. 163) but, nonetheless, he is disposed to talk. He orders Jane to entertain him but she has little to say. She is more concerned with surmising his character from his strong and arrogant looks (p. 164). Rochester declares that he is not ordering her about because she is a servant but because he is older than her, almost old enough, as he says, to be her father. This removal of the master–servant relationship on Rochester's part is an important moment in the book. It helps to place the emphasis on the personal relationship Rochester would like with Jane rather than on the professional one by which he employs her. Jane is slightly confused by this (p. 165) but she stands up to Rochester who is impressed by her frankness and personal strength (p. 166). He begins to present himself as a man who is hard because he has suffered greatly (p. 166). He was born to be kindly and he still wants to be, but circumstances have made him cold. He presents himself as a man whom fate has deprived of happiness (p. 167). Jane suggests that he try repenting and living a moral life. He pretends to scorn her lack of worldly wisdom, but it becomes clear (p. 168) that Jane has made a far deeper impact on him than he is prepared to admit. It is she, of course, who is the vision to whom he speaks and it is she for whom his heart will be the shrine. He promises to reform his way of life.

At this point Jane decides that it is Adèle's bedtime and gets up to attend to her. Mr Rochester asks Jane if she is afraid of him; she tells him she is not (p. 169). Rochester tells her that just as he is really a good man whom fate has hardened, so she is less austere and more passionate than she appears. Jane takes little notice, but it is clear to the observant reader not only that Jane's modesty and strength have begun to break through Rochester's shell of worldly wisdom, but that, in the strength of his love, he will be able to make her blossom into something more than the austere little schoolmistress she at present appears to be. Love, the deep calling of two natures to one another, will be the redemption of both Rochester and Jane. It will be a long time, however, before both of them can accept this, and when they do their hopes will be cruelly shattered. For the moment, however, Adèle comes rushing back into the room with her new clothes on; she reminds Rochester of her mother with whom he had the affair which began to turn his heart to dust.

CHAPTER 15, *pp. 172–82*

Rochester tells Jane about his affair with Adèle's mother. She was a dancer in the opera, called Céline Varens. Rochester was besotted with her but discovered she was not in love with him and was involved with another man, 'a young roué of a vicomte – a brainless and vicious youth' in Rochester's words. He describes to Jane the dramatic way in which he discovered Céline's infidelity.

Rochester explains that he doubts that Adèle is his child, as Céline maintained, but adds that out of human decency he took the child in when her mother abandoned her. Jane assures Rochester that she is not shocked by these revelations and indeed from now on will feel more sympathy for Adèle (p.176).

When Jane goes up to bed that night she lies awake thinking about Rochester and his obvious fondness for her. She is flattered by the manner in which he enjoys discussing his ideas with her, and feels that her life is becoming more interesting and meaningful: 'I ceased to pine after kindred; my thin crested destiny seemed to enlarge; the banks of existence were filled up; my bodily health improved; I gathered flesh and strength.' She realizes that Rochester has faults but considers him a basically good man. But she is puzzled by Rochester's attitude to Thornfield. She guesses there is something about the house which alienates him. Falling asleep, she is soon awakened by the sound of demonic laughter outside her bedroom. On her way to rouse Mrs Fairfax, Jane notices smoke billowing from Rochester's bedroom. Just in time she douses the flames with water and so saves her master's life. Rochester is strangely secretive about the causes of the fire. He disappears to the servants' quarters, presumably to reprimand Grace Poole, and when he returns he asks Jane not to mention the incident to anyone in the house, not even Mrs Fairfax. This frightening night-time adventure serves to bring Jane closer than ever to her master. She is obviously becoming infatuated with him, although her sense and judgement have not been swamped by these new, strong feelings. The whole scene forecasts, of course, the end of the novel and maintains the strong feeling of melodrama that characterizes it.

CHAPTER 16, *pp. 183–91*

Next morning Jane watches the servants clean Rochester's room and is amazed to see Grace Poole sewing rings onto new curtains. Could this be the woman who only the night before had caused the fire in Rochester's bedroom, laughing demonically as she did so? Jane is particularly puzzled because Grace looks so demure and unabashed. Deciding to question her closely, Jane is herself questioned by the servant, particularly as to whether she locks her door at night. Grace advises Jane to bolt her own door. Jane finds this astounding and it stimulates her imagination. Perhaps Rochester is so indulgent towards his potential murderess because she was once his mistress. This seems an unlikely explanation in view of Grace's plainness, and yet Rochester has appeared interested in Jane herself and, as she admits freely, she is herself no beauty.

As the day wears on Jane is impatient to see Rochester. She expects him to seek her out so that he can further explain the bewildering events of the previous night, and she hopes that he may unravel the deepening mystery of Grace Poole. However, by the end of the day, Jane learns the sad truth: her master has left Thornfield on the invitation of a Mr Eshton. At Eshton's home, 'the Leas', Mrs Fairfax explains, Lord Ingram and his two delightful daughters are being entertained. The daughters are called Mary and Blanche and Mrs Fairfax intimates that Mr Rochester has a special fondness for Blanche. She describes Blanche in great detail; and Jane feels that she has been deluding herself in thinking that her master could possibly prefer her to the splendidly beautiful and accomplished Blanche. So determined is she that her dangerous illusion of love should end that she formulates a plan: to draw her own portrait in chalk, being careful to be as realistic as possible, then to draw an imagined portrait of Blanche. Under her own portrait she plans to write the description: 'Portrait of a Governess, disconnected, poor and plain' and under the flattering portrait of Blanche, 'Blanche, an accomplished lady of rank' (p. 191).

It takes Jane a fortnight to draw Blanche's portrait. The drawing serves as a distraction from the inevitable loneliness Jane feels during

Rochester's absence. At the end of the chapter we see Jane at her most philosophical as she explains how it will be essential to maintain stoic calm during the eventful months ahead.

CHAPTER 17, *pp. 192–210*

Jane tries to bear Rochester's absence with stoicism, but when Mrs Fairfax suggests that he may disappear to the Continent for a year, she can hardly hide her 'sickening sense of disappointment'. Rallying her spirits, she contemplates advertising for another job, but not before Mrs Fairfax receives a letter from her master instructing her to make ready for an invasion of guests from 'the Leas'. During the next three days there are scenes of great activity at Thornfield. Jane cannot help noticing Grace Poole's sinister form gliding about the house, and she overhears a conversation between Leah and one of the char-women, the substance of which is that Grace earns a comparatively large sum of money for whatever mysterious job she does (p. 194). Jane realizes that she has purposely been excluded from the mystery of Thornfield.

Excitement mounts as the time draws near for the arrival of the guests. Adèle is particularly happy, for here at last is a real opportunity for her to dress up and join in some glamorous fun.

Mr Rochester is observed riding towards Thornfield alongside a purple clad Blanche Ingram, and for the rest of the evening, while the guests dine, Jane has to restrain an agitated Adèle from bursting into the party. There is a poignant moment when Jane listens to the murmur of song and conversation downstairs, trying to discern Rochester's voice (p. 198).

The following day, the fine ladies and gentlemen make an excursion, and once more Jane notices that Blanche and Rochester ride together. Mrs Fairfax informs Jane that Rochester requires her to accompany Adèle into the drawing-room after dinner. Jane is very nervous, but on Mrs Fairfax's suggestion ensconces herself and her charge in a nook of the room before the dazzling party arrive. Jane describes the guests in some detail, but reserves particular emphasis for Blanche. She is certainly as attractive as her description has merited; but, asks Jane, could Mr Rochester like such a woman? She appears haughty, pompous and unkind. Jane, however, will reserve judgement until she sees Blanche and Rochester together. When Rochester appears, Jane all but swoons with a mixture of joy and pain. She tells herself again that he is not handsome, yet admits for the first time that she is in love: 'I had not intended to love him ... He made me love him without looking at me.' She feels that they have a bond between them that defies logic, age and class. It becomes clear that Jane's adoration of Rochester is both physical and emotional.

The presence of Adèle prompts Blanche to make some spiteful remarks about governesses. Bored with this subject, Blanche then commands Rochester to sing with her, flattering him the while with her views on the young men of the day. She makes it quite clear that she despises a man who is interested in his appearance, as it would obviously serve to deflect some of the glory away from her own beauty. Jane listens to Blanche and Rochester sing together and then slips away, as she hopes, unnoticed. Rochester follows her, however, and perceives her misery. His concern for her well-being is obvious, and he makes it clear that he wishes her to join his guests every evening of their stay at Thornfield.

CHAPTER 18, *pp. 211–24*

Filled with guests Thornfield is a merry place and the spring weather is warm and sunny. When rainier days persist, indoor entertainment is invented, including a game of charades. One evening Jane watches while Rochester and Blanche Ingram play the principals in a three-act charade. Ironically, the first act involves a detailed marriage scene between Rochester and a magnificent Miss Ingram. While the other guests perform their charade, Jane finds herself interested solely in the interchanges between her master and his 'new bride'. Their whisperings and mutual confidences cause Jane discomfort because,

as she explains: 'I had learnt to love Mr Rochester: I could not un-
love him now ... because I saw all his attentions appropriated by
a great lady, who scorned to touch me with the hem of her robes
as she passed.' However, this pain is not compounded of jealousy,
as it is clear that Jane thinks very little of Blanche Ingram (p.
215). Jane concedes that Rochester will marry Blanche (as she is now
sure that the match will go ahead) for her wealth and her social con-
nections, but not for love, because from close observation Jane realizes
that Rochester is not charmed by his potential bride. Knowing her
master well, Jane sees that the way to his heart is not through showy
and superficial vitality. Rightly she suspects that he hates pretension
and, as we see, Blanche is the very personification of pretension. Jane
is now so deeply in love that she no longer concedes Rochester's faults.
She simply longs to get to the bottom of the mystery surrounding
Rochester and Thornfield, a mystery which she realizes causes her
master such unhappiness.

One day, a certain gloom descends on the company due to
Rochester's absence. However, someone soon appears to enliven the
party. It is Mr Mason, and Jane takes an instant dislike to him. She
cannot understand what he and her master might have had in common
for, as Mason explains, they are old friends: 'the contrast could not
be much greater between a sleek gander and a fierce falcon: between
a meek sheep and the rough coated, keen-eyed dog, its guardian.'
By and by Jane learns that Mason comes from the West Indies. This
puzzles her as she has not heard Rochester mention travelling so far
afield. The suspense and melodrama deepen.

Presently there is another diversion. A footman brings word that
an old gypsy woman from the nearby encampment has visited the
house 'to tell the gentry their fortunes'. This stirs Blanche's imagination and, much against her mother's wishes, she commands that the
gypsy be brought into the drawing-room to amuse the party. The
gypsy is strangely impervious to Miss Ingram's haughty demands,
however, and insists on seeing the young and single ladies one by
one, in the adjoining library. Blanche is the first to have her fortune
told. She returns rather subdued and, as Jane observes, becomes
steadily more gloomy and sour. Mary Ingram, Amy and Louisa Eshton
are too frightened to see the old hag alone, so they go together amidst

much giggling. As the girls are recounting their visit to the rest of the party, the footman tells Jane that the gypsy wishes to see her, too. Unafraid to go into the library alone, Jane enters the gypsy's den, consumed with curiosity.

CHAPTER 19, *pp.* 225–34

The gypsy seems surprised that Jane is so bold and inquisitive. She begins to question Jane and discovers that the girl's ambition is to open a school and run it herself. This is scorned by the gypsy who asks whether Jane does not long for matrimony. This leads her to ask what Jane thinks of the proposed match between Rochester and Blanche Ingram. Jane is very non-committal, especially as to whether it is indeed a love match. The gypsy acknowledges that she has had to tell Blanche that Rochester is not as rich as he seems, and the old woman intimates that Blanche's disappointment may well cloud the couple's future happiness. Impatiently, Jane requests the gypsy to concentrate upon her, which the old woman duly does, studying Jane's face with a passionate interest, and pronouncing her discoveries with an articulate expression rather out of tune with the character of a wandering gypsy.

Sure enough, Jane learns that the gypsy is none other than Mr Rochester who has inveigled her into a private charade. Jane is relieved to recall that she has not given away any secrets about herself, and has indeed learnt more than she has imparted. She informs Rochester of Mr Mason's arrival and is amazed to see her master's bold façade crumble before her eyes. Still employing the language of charade and enigma, Rochester intimates that this visit may portend evil, or at least alienation from his friends and guests. He asks Jane if she would stand by him if all others desert. Jane assures him that she would do all she could to comfort him. Later on she overhears Rochester showing Mason to his room, and is relieved by her master's cheerful and relaxed tone of voice.

CHAPTER 20, *pp. 235–48*

Jane wakes to hear a blood-curdling scream from the bedroom above, followed by the sounds of struggling and of a man shouting for help. The whole household is now awake, and the women particularly are terrified. Eventually Rochester appears and attempts to set their minds at rest with the tale of a servant girl screaming from a nightmare. Jane is not convinced by Rochester's explanation, and waits in her bedroom in case her assistance is required. As she expects, Rochester knocks at her door and, without attempting to calm her with soothing explanations, asks her to bring a sponge and smelling salts, and inquires whether she is frightened of blood. He then takes her up to the dreaded third floor and into a tapestry-hung room. Jane hears the terrible sound of what she has come to recognize as Grace Poole's inimitable demonic laugh. Mason is slumped in a chair, his arm and shoulder soaked in blood. Rochester asks Jane to stay with the injured man, bathing his wounds and applying the smelling salts, while he collects the local surgeon. Before he disappears, he commands Mason not to talk to Jane.

For two hours Jane keeps her lonely and terrifying vigil. During this time she worries away at the many mysteries connected with Thornfield. Eventually Rochester and the surgeon arrive and from the conversation of the three men it emerges that a woman (could it be Grace Poole?) has attacked Mason not only with a knife, but with her teeth also. Rochester is obviously eager to get Mason away from the house, and as soon as the wounded man is bandaged and dressed he leaves with the surgeon in a carriage. Rochester guides Jane to the garden. Here he admits that he finds Thornfield too horrible to re-enter: 'that house is a mere dungeon'. Rochester does not really explain the appalling events of that night to Jane. He simply admits that: 'To live, for me, Jane, is to stand on a crater crust which may crack and spew fire any day' (p. 245).

Mason, Rochester explains, is not a direct threat to him, but he could destroy Rochester's happiness. He then tells Jane a form of parable concerning a young man who makes an error early in life and must then repent and suffer for his error for the rest of his days (p. 247). Jane's reply shows she is not yet strong enough to guess at the saving power of human love.

CHAPTER 21, *pp. 249–68*

Jane has some strange dreams about tending a small child which she recognizes as a presentiment of suffering and even death. Sure enough, Bessie's husband, Robert Leaven, appears at Thornfield with terrible news about the Reeds at Gateshead. John has committed suicide, ruined by debt. Mrs Reed has had a stroke and is lying on her death bed. Apparently, Mrs Reed wants to see Jane before she dies. Jane cannot refuse the dying woman this request and so asks Mr Rochester's permission to make the hundred mile journey to Gateshead. This is the first time that Jane has mentioned her relations, and Rochester is surprised to hear of his little governess's past life. He is also sad to see Jane go, and anxious about her journeying so far. He is determined that she shall have some extra money for her stay.

Jane takes this opportunity to question her master a little more closely about his plans for her and Adèle once he has married Miss Ingram. Jane suggests that Adèle go to school. Rochester agrees that Blanche would surely 'walk over her [Adèle] rather too emphatically' were the two to share his attentions. But Rochester is horrified to hear Jane's plan of advertising for a new post, and begs her to leave such arrangements to him.

The next day Jane arrives at Gateshead. Bessie is welcoming, yet Jane cannot help but remember the misery she has endured in the house and the cruel hostility which drove her away. Yet she is pleased to discover that 'the gaping wound of my wrongs, too, was now quite healed; the flame of resentment extinguished'. She is amazed to meet Georgiana and Eliza again. Georgiana has grown as plump and languid as her sister has become thin and austere. The sisters are rude and haughty towards their cousin, but Jane is unmoved and simply asks to see their mother, deciding that her visit cannot be a brief one and that she must in some way tie up the loose ends of her past.

Towards the invalid Mrs Reed, Jane is gentle and mild, even when the woman turns her face away in an imperious manner. Gradually, however, Mrs Reed unbends and begins to explain her past resentment towards Jane. Apparently her husband had loved Jane's mother, his sister, very dearly, and when she married beneath her station had stuck by her loyally even to the point of taking in her child when the poor woman died. Mr Reed had loved Jane in a way which enraged his wife; she suspected that he loved the baby girl more than he did his own children. It is clear that Mrs Reed would have sent Jane to a workhouse rather than have her in her own home, which was why her husband's dying wish that Jane be brought up with the Reed children was so particularly galling. Mrs Reed then lapses into fevered ravings. Her health takes a turn for the worse and for the next ten days Jane is unable to resume her ministry of absolution. We see, however, how far she has developed from the opening chapters. She is capable of pity now.

In the meantime she is ignored by the Reed girls until they see her sketching. Among other sketches is a faithful portrait of Mr Rochester which serves to assuage the loneliness Jane inevitably feels whilst away from Thornfield. A conversation about this and the other sketches serves to break the ice between the three girls, and Georgiana in particular seems to take Jane into her confidence, describing her experiences during the London season and pouring out her woes at being confined in such a depressing place as Gateshead. Eliza gives herself no time for complaining as she is extraordinarily active, filling every minute of the day with tasks. She tells Jane that she longs to escape from Gateshead too, only unlike her sister who wishes to rejoin the excitement of social life, she hopes to 'seek a retirement where punctual habits would be permanently secured from disturbance'.

Jane revisits Mrs Reed and learns the real reason why she has been summoned to attend the woman's death bed. Apparently, three years previously Mrs Reed had received a letter from Jane's uncle in Madeira, announcing his intention to leave his entire fortune to Jane. Still smarting from Jane's childish, yet accurate testimonial of hatred towards her, Mrs Reed decides to punish Jane from afar by informing John Eyre, the girl's uncle, that Jane had died of typhus fever at Lowood School. Jane freely forgives her aunt, but still the sad and twisted woman cannot unbend towards the girl she has hated for so long. Shortly afterwards Mrs Reed dies. Her daughters are hardly moved by the demise of their mother.

CHAPTER 22, *pp. 269–75*

Both Georgiana and Eliza persuade Jane to stay longer at Gateshead; Georgiana because she sorely needs some sympathetic help while she comes to terms with her mother's death and her sister's cold indifference; Eliza, because she wishes to share with Jane (whom she now considers a worthy friend) her plans for the future. The place where she has planned to move, which is so conveniently immune from worldly irritations, turns out to be a nunnery in France. Jane now discloses that this is indeed where her cousin goes, rising, in time, to be Mother Superior. Georgiana, apparently, makes a reasonable marriage to a 'wealthy worn out man of fashion'. The fate of both girls is pitifully loveless.

Jane has mixed feelings about returning to Thornfield. She is anxious to see Mr Rochester, yet realizes that her future as his servant, confidante and helper is limited because of his forthcoming marriage to Miss Ingram. She decides to walk from the village of Millcote to Thornfield, and as she nears the house she sees Rochester sitting on a stile, writing. He is obviously delighted to see Jane, and they soon resume their affectionate teasing of one another. Jane is so moved by her master's gentleness towards her that she takes the opportunity to thank him for giving her the first real home she has had during her troubled life (p. 274).

Adèle too is delighted at Jane's return, and there is a touching picture of cosy and domestic comfort, made particularly poignant by the shadows cast by Rochester's marriage which will exile Jane and Adèle from the 'sunshine of his presence' (p. 274).

Throughout the next fortnight, Jane tries to discover whether this marriage is as imminent as she suspects. Both she and Mrs Fairfax are puzzled by Rochester's apparent lack of interest in Blanche Ingram, and although Jane is glad to be back in her master's favour, his interest in her only increases the tension she feels because of her love for him and her fears of life without him.

CHAPTER 23, *pp. 276–85*

It is midsummer at Thornfield and the weather is perfect. On Midsummer's Eve itself Jane wanders out into the garden marvelling at its peace and beauty. She senses the presence of Mr Rochester and tries to escape from the garden before he spies her. She is too late, however: she and her beloved master fall into conversation. How sad, muses Rochester, that Jane has to leave Thornfield because of his impending marriage to Blanche Ingram. Although his tone is sarcastic, Jane believes that she must indeed leave the house and her new-found friends. When Rochester tells her that he has found his governess a new post in Ireland with the dreadful sounding Mrs Dionysius O'Gall of Bitternutt Lodge, Jane does not suspect a strong element of make-believe and mockery. Instead she breaks down. She declares that she cannot bear the idea of not seeing Rochester again. Tearfully she admits that her stay at Thornfield has been one of the bright spots of her life (p. 281). But most of all, she has appreciated her friendship with Rochester. Moved by Jane's declaration, Rochester begins to admit that his plan to marry Blanche is only a smokescreen, and that it is Jane whom he loves and wishes to marry. Apparently Blanche and her mother were horrified to learn that Rochester's fortune was not as great as they imagined (a false rumour spread by Rochester to test Blanche's real feelings). Jane can hardly believe what is happening. As if to prove Rochester's true feelings, she scrutinizes his face in the moonlight, and, satisfying herself that he is not playing sarcastic games with her, consents to be his wife. Blissfully happy, they remain in the garden entwined in one another's arms, until a freak storm whips up and torrential rain soaks them to the skin. A sinister note is sounded when the chestnut tree makes a curious moaning sound as the wind rushes through its branches.

Next morning Jane hears that the tree has been struck by lightning and half of it burnt away. The sudden violence and savagery of the storm has its echoes in Rochester's wild relief that Jane has consented to marry him; had she not been so blinded by love, she admits that she would have wondered at his behaviour, and certainly questioned his repeated defiance of Fate, and his imprecations to God that what he plans to do has his forgiveness and sanction. The reader's pleasure at Jane's happiness cannot but be chilled by the growing presentiment that an even greater storm is gathering and that it will be some time before Jane and Rochester can be at peace together. We glimpse a moment of great tenderness horribly threatened by foreboding.

CHAPTER 24, *pp. 286–302*

Jane can hardly believe the events of the previous night, and she longs to see Rochester again so that he can put her mind at rest. Since his declaration of love for her she has blossomed and, when she does see her master after breakfast, he remarks on her beautiful face and adds that he has arranged for the family jewels to be sent to Thornfield, so that he can further enhance her beauty. Jane is adamant that she does not wish to be turned into 'an ape in a harlequin's jacket – a jay in borrowed plumes'. Undeterred, Rochester outlines his plans for their honeymoon: they are to travel to his favourite European haunts: 'where-ever I stamped my Hoof, your sylph's foot shall step also' (p. 288).

They discuss their love for one another. Rochester admits that although he has had experience of many women, Jane is the only one who has truly captured his heart while retaining a 'sense of pliancy' and gentleness. As if to test just how smitten her future husband really is, Jane asks him a favour. It is obvious that Rochester dreads Jane questioning him about the mystery surrounding Grace Poole, and so is greatly relieved when Jane merely wishes to know why he made her believe he was planning to marry Blanche Ingram. He replies that it was a device to make Jane jealous and thus fan her love for him. As to Blanche's feelings, he assures Jane that they 'are concentrated in one – pride'. Jane then asks Rochester another favour: to explain to a bemused Mrs Fairfax that he plans to marry not Blanche but his little governess. Mrs Fairfax had witnessed Jane and Rochester arriving back from their moonlight courtship the previous night, and it is obvious that she is shocked.

Rochester keeps his word and Jane visits the old housekeeper, only to have a rather dispiriting conversation with her. Mrs Fairfax at first admits that she finds the match faintly preposterous, then issues Jane with world-weary warnings (p. 293).

Overcome with doubts, her happiness deeply threatened, Jane goes with Rochester to Millcote to select dresses for the wedding trousseau. Adèle accompanies them, and Rochester spins her a delightful tale, comparing Jane to a fairy who steals his heart away and, with a magic talisman (a wedding ring), makes all things possible. In this rather childish story we see clearly Rochester's yearning for happiness, and how he sees Jane as someone imbued with the magical qualities (first a fairy, now an angel) which will redeem his misspent youth. Jane and Rochester do not agree on a choice of fabrics. Jane prefers plainer designs, Rochester would seem to want her in dazzling colours and rich silks. Jane's chief concern is that by becoming Rochester's wife, penniless as she is, she will lose her independence and become more like his slave girl than his wife. She then remembers her uncle in Madeira and the inheritance that he wished to settle upon her, and determines to write to him. With these longings for independence Jane is careful, during the next few weeks leading up to her marriage, not to submit to Rochester. He sings her a sentimental love song one evening and she mocks it. She takes care not to presume upon her future change of status and continues to carry out her duties as governess with diligence. Indeed she only sees Rochester for a few hours after dinner when she teases and fights with him. Although he now calls her his 'malicious elf' instead of his 'darling', Jane realizes that this suits his crusty temperament more than a sickly-sweet courtship, and her flirtatious sparring with him can only keep Rochester on his mettle and retain his interest. At the end of the chapter, however, Jane admits that she is more than ever madly in love with Rochester, and this love has supplanted her love of God. The confession is an important one.

CHAPTER 25, *pp. 303–14*

It is the day before the wedding. Jane looks at the trunks packed for the honeymoon, labelled Mrs Rochester. She cannot bring herself to believe that such happiness can be hers. Agitated and missing Rochester (who has had to go away for the day on business) Jane wanders in the garden. She gazes at the mournful sight of the dead and blackened chestnut tree, then is frightened to see that the moon is a threatening blood red colour. As the evening wears on, Jane becomes more and more nervous and, having made a fire in Rochester's study so that the room is cosy for his arrival, she rushes out into the stormy night to meet him as he rides back. He is amazed to see Jane striding towards him in the cold and wet and he is concerned at her agitation. After supper together in his study, Jane explains her odd behaviour. The previous night, she tells Rochester, she had a terrifying experience. First she dreamt that she was trying to follow Rochester down a long winding road. Her progress was impeded by pelting rain and a small child moaning piteously whom she was compelled to look after. In the second dream she was still holding the helpless child in her arms, but this time they are in the ruins of what was once Thornfield Hall. Sensing that Rochester was riding away from her, Jane climbed up to the top of the crumbling building, and sure enough, she could see her beloved disappearing into the distance. As she strained forward for a final look at Rochester, the wall crumbled, the child fell out of her grasp, and she awoke terror-stricken.

Once awake, Jane experiences something more real than a dream, but no less terrifying. Someone has her wedding veil and is gazing at it in the light of a candle. At first Jane thinks it must be Sophie, Adèle's maid. Then she realizes that she has never seen this woman before, and although she immediately connects night-time horrors with

Grace Poole, the spectre is definitely not Grace. With its red eyes and tangled black hair it looks more like a vampire. After ripping the veil in two, the woman stares malignantly at Jane, until the poor girl faints with terror (p. 312).

Rochester tries to persuade Jane that this 'vampire' was as much a dream as the crying child and the ruined Thornfield Hall. However, when Jane tells him that in the morning she indeed found the veil torn in two on her bedroom floor, his attitude changes. Rochester insists that Jane spend that night in Adèle's nursery, and lock the door. Jane does as Rochester advises, but she cannot sleep. Filled with such a mixture of happiness and dire presentiments, she greets her wedding morning with dread.

You should note again how skilfully melodrama is used to heighten the excitement and the reader's intuition that there cannot yet be a happy ending.

CHAPTER 26, *pp. 315–24*

Jane dresses for her wedding, urged by Rochester not to delay. Rochester is indeed determined that the ceremony be started as soon as possible, and he rushes Jane to the church with almost indecent haste.

As they enter the church Jane notices two figures lurking by the gravestones, and concludes that they are parishioners curious to witness the wedding. The two figures enter the church, following Jane and her bridegroom. As the wedding service commences she is dimly aware of them watching from the back of the church. When the clergyman reaches the point in the service where he asks if there is anyone who has 'just impediment', one of the figures from the back of the church declares that he indeed has reason for the marriage not to take place. Although Rochester attempts to force the clergyman to continue with the service, the stranger is insistent. He announces that Rochester already has a wife. On further questioning it appears that the stranger is a solicitor, Mr Briggs, and that he has proof of

Rochester's marriage as well as a witness. The witness is none other than the mysterious Mr Mason of the West Indies, Mr Rochester's brother-in-law. This is one of the most dramatic moments in the book. The reader has been wishing happiness for Jane but has been warned in a melodramatic way that this cannot be. Cold, blunt reality now intrudes. Happiness evaporates with the appalling suggestion (particularly for Charlotte Brontë's contemporaries) of bigamy.

Rochester admits everything. He intended to commit bigamy, yet, he brazens out, his wife is a lunatic, holed up at Thornfield, and is more like an animal than a human being. He commands that the assembled company in the church follow him to Thornfield to see for themselves what sort of woman he has been married to for fifteen years. He appeals to the witnesses, and to the reader, for compassion. He tries to insist that our feelings for him as a man should be stronger than conventional morality. In part they are.

Jane, Rochester, Mason, Briggs and the clergyman enter the bedroom where Jane had nursed Mason after he had been so appallingly attacked. Through a second door Grace Poole is seen, and behind her, a horrific, bestial creature growling like a mad dog. When this creature sees Rochester it sets upon him, almost strangling him in fury. Rochester introduces the demented being as his wife, Bertha Mason, and with savage irony compares her to Jane who can only stand by in mute horror.

As they leave Grace Poole and her awful charge, Briggs explains to Jane that her letter to her uncle announcing her forthcoming marriage became known to Mason. John Eyre was mortified that his niece might be in danger of contracting a bigamous marriage, and quickly despatched Mason to England to stop it. Briggs assures Jane that she is guilty of nothing. Finding the opportunity, Jane speedily escapes into the sanctum of her bedroom, and experiences a feeling of almost total numbness. Her hopes and dreams have been dashed, and, most painful of all, she realizes that the man she most loved and trusted in the world has destroyed her confidence. Her life seems shattered. She is a woman alone in the world. She summons up enough strength to decide to leave Thornfield as soon as possible; and to ask God, whom she has ignored somewhat of late, to help her in her hour of need.

CHAPTER 27, *pp. 325–48*

On the afternoon of her wedding day, Jane wakes to misery. She realizes she is alone and must depend on her own strength to survive.

Rochester is outside her bedroom door. He carries her downstairs and attempts to revive her. She reads in his face agony at what has happened. She knows she still loves him, but knows also that she must leave him. She cannot, of course, defy the conventions of her day. Rochester frantically pours out his plans for her. Thornfield is to be shut up, only Bertha Mason and Grace Poole remaining in residence. Jane is to be transported to the South of France, away from prying eyes and malicious tongues. Jane replies that if she were to live like that, then she would be nothing more than Rochester's mistress. Even more frantic, Rochester begs her to hear him out. As if in defence he offers her a lurid, yet obviously true, account of his forced marriage to Bertha and of how he discovered her madness, left her and fruitlessly roved Europe in search of joy (pp. 332–9). Then, he explains, something very akin to a miracle occurred. He met Jane. He knew instantly that, despite her plain appearance, her youth, her lack of sophistication, she was the woman for him, the woman he had been searching for all these years. Terrified lest Jane's very qualities of honesty and purity should forbid her to marry bigamously, let alone become his mistress, Rochester decided he must hide the truth of Bertha's existence. When all is told, Rochester pleads with Jane to stay with him. Without her his life is not worth living. He begs her to break the laws of society so that she can save his life. Jane is tempted, especially as she considers her loved one's very real misery. Yet she knows that she must retain her self-respect and that this self-respect can only come from obeying what she believes is right. For Jane, personal happiness must be found within the laws and conventions of society. She knows this instinctively. For the reader, Rochester's confession of his unhappiness in his illicit love affairs proves this point. It is highly significant that when he finds the woman he truly loves his impulses are all towards marriage. He sees now that Jane is right to hold with virtue and convention. He sadly admits that to make Jane his mistress, and in the process destroy her pride and independence, would be like imprisoning a wild creature. Rochester respects Jane's moral strength and declares that it is this inner self that he loves, her 'will, and energy and virtue and purity' not merely her 'brittle frame'. He allows her to depart, leaving him with his shattered dreams (p. 345).

That night Jane has a dream in which a female form emerges from the moon and begs her to 'flee temptation'. Rising before dawn, Jane packs a few essentials, as much money as she has in the world and, without allowing herself to say goodbye to anyone at Thornfield, walks out into the summer dawn. Almost dead with misery, she boards a coach and asks the driver to take her as far as her money will allow, as far away as possible from Rochester and temptation.

CHAPTER 28, *pp. 349–64*

Two days later, the driver of the coach drops Jane at a crossroads. The nearest town is ten miles away. From its name, Jane realizes that she is in the North Midlands. She decides to spend the night on the heathland, protected by what she imagines to be the benign force of Mother Nature. Tortured by the thought of Rochester's suffering, Jane prays to God to protect him and, satisfied that her prayer is answered, falls into a deep sleep (p. 351).

The next morning the full extent of her predicament strikes her. She must find food and water or she will starve, however peaceful and seemingly plenteous the surrounding countryside appears to be. She comes across a small village and steels herself to ask for employment. The woman serving in the bakery is very discouraging. There appears to be no hope of a job. Jane asks the same question at a house on the outskirts of the village, and again at the vicarage. By now Jane is famished and returns to the bakery to beg for a cake or some bread in exchange for a silk handkerchief and her gloves. She is sternly rebuffed but she is saved from complete starvation by a hunk of bread begged from a farmer that night, and next morning by some cold and congealed porridge about to be thrown out of a cottage. The thought of another night outside drives Jane to pursue a distant light she sees through trees. The light comes from a cottage, and inside we glimpse a cosy scene. Two young women and what appears to be their elderly housekeeper sit around a flickering fire. The two girls are translating passages from a German book and chatting about the recent death of their father and the expected return of their brother, St John. As Hannah the housekeeper begins to prepare supper, Jane remembers her own desperate condition and knocks on the door. She is brusquely turned away by Hannah, who believes she must have some evil reason for hanging around the house so late at night. Jane believes that her last moments have come. She has no more strength to suffer further rejections, and she offers herself up to the will of God.

Her despairing words are heard by St John as he approaches the house. Sensing that she is no ordinary beggar, he brings her inside and Jane is revived with warm milk and bread, a comfortable seat by the fire, and the obvious concern of St John and his sisters, Mary and Diana. Jane will tell them nothing of herself, only disclose that her name is Jane Elliott, an alias she had already prepared. Respecting her need to recover her strength before recounting her life history, the Rivers family prepare a warm bed for their guest, and Jane sleeps properly for the first time in several days.

CHAPTER 29, *pp. 365–75*

Jane lies in a fatigued stupor for three days, dimly aware of the visits of St John and his sisters. On the third day, Jane feels strong enough to go downstairs and there meets Hannah who questions her fairly closely about her begging. Hannah is obviously puzzled that someone so 'book learned' as Jane should be so destitute. Jane reproaches the housekeeper for having turned her away simply because she thought the girl was destitute (p. 369). Hannah explains that she acted so because she feels as responsible as a mother for the Rivers children.

They have no parents, and Hannah has been with the family for thirty years. Now that they have both explained the reasons for their behaviour that first evening, Jane and Hannah make up and shake hands with civility and friendship.

Hannah proceeds to tell Jane something about the Rivers family history. The family is a respectable one, and had been 'gentry i'th'owd days o'th'Henrys'. Unfortunately, old Mr Rivers was swindled out of the only money he had, and thus his children have to fend for themselves – the sisters as governesses, and St John as a parson, for which he obviously has a real vocation. The children were very fond of the family house, Marsh End, and the parish of Morton, and Diana and Mary were particularly sad at having to work away from home and be parted from each other and their brother.

When Diana and Mary return from their walk, they make Jane comfortable in the parlour. St John is there reading, and Jane gets a chance to study him. He is a handsome man, although rather hard and stern. He begins to question Jane after tea, and asks if she has any relatives he can write to. Jane reveals that she is an orphan, and briefly sketches in her life history. She does not mention Rochester and simply says that she has had to leave her employment in a great hurry which explains her lack of possessions and shabby appearance. She thanks the Riverses for their kindness, although she neatly draws a comparison between the sisters' 'spontaneous, genuine and genial compassion' and their brother's 'evangelical charity'. This distinction, as we shall see, is an important one. St John promises that he will try to find some suitable employment for Jane but that being poor himself he cannot necessarily conjure up a grand job. Jane assures him she will do anything to earn her keep, and with that the conversation ends.

CHAPTER 30, *pp. 376–84*

Jane becomes very close to the Rivers sisters. She is stimulated by their intellectual pursuits and charmed by their obvious love for the surrounding countryside. Jane is particularly fond of Diana and basks in the girl's vivacity and intelligence. But St John has none of his sisters' love of life. His work in the parish is carried out in a spirit of stern duty, and he seems to equate the family home and the moors with gloom. These observations are borne out when Jane hears St John preaching (p. 378). Jane feels very strongly that the parson has not found peace with God and is involved in a grim struggle with his soul and conscience.

Soon the time draws near when Diana and Mary must return to their posts as governesses and St John lock up Marsh End and return to the parsonage at Morton. Jane asks whether he has given further thought to her need for employment. He has indeed formulated a plan, but he doubts whether, with Jane's obvious love of life, she will want such employment. It transpires that he founded a school for poor boys in Morton a while ago and now has plans, with financial help from Miss Oliver, a rich local heiress, for a similar school for girls. The school needs a mistress. Would Jane find it too boring? Jane replies that she would be glad of such a job and thinks to herself that to be buried in the depths of the countryside would at least serve as a 'safe asylum' from Mr Rochester. St John prophesies that Jane will not stay in Morton for long. He recognizes her restless spirit and admits that he shares her yearning nature and desire for change and interest. Indeed, he has already hinted that now his father is dead he will not remain Morton's parson for more than a year. Diana also intimates that she and her sister may be saying farewell to their brother for a very long time, maybe even for ever.

As the sisters weep softly at the prospect of their lonely fate, St John announces that he has received another piece of sad news. Their uncle John has died and has left his fortune of twenty thousand pounds to another relative. He has left St John, Diana and Mary a mere thirty guineas to be divided between them for the purchase of mourning rings. Even a thousand pounds each would have enabled the sisters and their brother to remain together. With much sadness, the sisters leave Marsh End and Jane, St John and Hannah move to Morton parsonage.

CHAPTER 31, *pp. 385–91*

Jane settles into her new life as a schoolmistress and although she finds the village children rather crude and intractable, she realizes that it will be satisfying to kindle their interest in learning. She compares her present life in her bare, clean, yet rather comfortless cottage to the life she could have had in the South of France as Rochester's mistress. She is not unaware that this life would have offered many joys, not least to bask in Rochester's love for her; yet she knows that she has made the right choice, for as a 'slave in a fool's paradise' she would have been constantly haunted by a sense of guilt; and she would prefer to be a 'village schoolmistress, free and honest, in a breezy mountain nook in the healthy heart of England', however lonely and however tormented by unconsummated love.

St John interrupts her musings; he notices that she has been crying and asks whether she is happy in her new work. Jane intimates that she is happy to have made a virtuous decision, and St John sympathizes with the burden of her struggle. He, too, has had to 'control the workings of inclination' when assailed by doubts as to his suitability as a parson. Then, out of the darkness, came the inspiration to be a missionary: strength and self-respect flooded back (p. 388). St John confides that he has indeed made plans to leave England for the East within a year. However, the young man has a visitor who, by her startling beauty, almost disarms his austerity. Miss Rosamond Oliver is the young heiress whose money has helped establish Jane's little school. Jane is overcome by Rosamond's physical perfection and comes near to envy when she considers her good luck at being wealthy as well as beautiful: 'What happy combination of the planets presided over her birth, I wonder?' St John is also moved by the lovely young woman, yet he seems to have made a resolution not to be seduced by her beauty. When she asks him to pay a visit to her father's home that evening, he forces himself to refuse. Jane watches with amazement as Rosamond beseeches St John, flirts with him, and charms him. St John walks away from both women 'inexorable as death', in his sister Diana's words.

CHAPTER 32, *pp. 392–402*

Jane begins to find satisfaction in her work at the school, and indeed
earns the admiration of the local Morton people. Yet, amidst the calm
of her well ordered life, Jane is still haunted by visions of Rochester,
and tortured by pangs of love. As if to take her mind off her own
unhappiness, Jane becomes interested in the relationship between
Rosamond Oliver and St John. Rosamond often calls at the school
when she thinks she might meet St John, and her love for him is
clear. Clear, too, is the sway she holds over the blushing young parson.
Yet Jane realizes that he will not relinquish his missionary plans for
a mere love-affair. Jane is, on the whole, complimentary about
Rosamond, although hints of intellectual snobbery abound (p. 394).
Rosamond is charmed by Jane's talent for sketching, and persuades
her to paint her portrait. Jane is invited to the Oliver mansion and
discovers that Mr Oliver thinks highly of the Rivers family and would
welcome a match between St John and his lovely daughter (p. 395).

Jane intends to acquaint St John with this information when he
visits her on Guy Fawkes' afternoon. She shows him her portrait of
Rosamond and offers to paint him a miniature version to take on
his travels to the East. Growing bolder, Jane then suggests that St
John should marry the subject of the portrait; after all, Rosamond
clearly adores him, and her father would be delighted at the match.
St John is pleased to share his feelings with Jane and admits that
although he is physically attracted to the girl, he knows she would
not make, in his own words, a 'good wife'. St John is far too pragmatic
to risk his life's work, his ambitions, his vocation, for the sake of
a passion which may fade. He describes himself as a 'cold, hard man'
– yet this cold, hard man mysteriously tears a narrow slip from the
margin of the portrait when he thinks Jane is not looking. Jane is
genuinely puzzled.

CHAPTER 33, *pp. 403–14*

After St John leaves the weather closes in. Snow continues to fall
the following day and as Jane sits at her fireside she reads a poem
St John has given her. Some time later she is astonished to open
the door to St John and is perturbed lest something terrible has dragged
him away from his home on such a stormy, snowy night. She tries
to discover the reasons for his visit but he is singularly uncommuni-
cative, and Jane grows tired of having to make small talk. Suddenly,
St John announces that he is going to tell Jane a story, and proceeds
to relate Jane's life history, even to the details of her near marriage
to Rochester (p. 405). Apparently, Rochester has been frantically
searching for Jane, placing advertisements in local papers, and contact-
ing district parsons. Jane is only interested in the well-being of Mr
Rochester, and when St John can give her no news she fears he may
have left England for a dissolute life on the Continent. But how did
St John know that the friendless orphan Jane Elliott was indeed Jane
Eyre, lately of Thornfield Hall? It appears that on the strip of paper
he had stolen from Rosamond's portrait, Jane had unwittingly signed
her name. St John now delivers another piece of stunning news. He
has learnt from the solicitor, Briggs, that John Eyre, Jane's uncle in
Madeira, has left all his fortune to her: twenty thousand pounds. Jane
receives the news with shock; shock mingled with pleasure and
solemnity in equal measures (p. 407). Such an enormous sum of money
will require a lot of managing. Jane is genuinely bewildered that Briggs
should have written to St John informing him of her bequest. How
did he know that she would be living with the Rivers family? St John
has to have the mystery prised out of him, but when he admits, by
way of explanation, that his real name is St John Eyre Rivers, the
links in the chain seem to join together. Jane's uncle in Madeira was
the brother of St John's mother. Jane has miraculously acquired three
cousins. This revelation fills her with intense joy. Instantly she realizes
how she can help her three cousins stay together as a family. She
will divide her inheritance equally between them, enabling Diana and
Mary to leave their jobs, and St John to marry Miss Oliver. If St

John agrees, Jane's pleasure will be 'delicious', for as she explains, 'repaying, in part, a mighty obligation, and winning to myself life long friends' will bring her more satisfaction than being a rich and lonely woman. She declares that she will never want to marry. After a long argument, St John eventually overcomes his scruples, and arrangements are made to share out Jane's fortune.

CHAPTER 34, *pp. 415–35*

It is Christmas time, and Jane has closed the school and bidden fond farewell to her pupils. St John asks Jane what she intends to do now she is no longer tied to the job of schoolmistress. Indeed, since hearing of her fortune, St John has found a replacement for Jane at Morton School. Jane replies that she wants to renovate the parsonage so that when Diana and Mary return for Christmas it will be to a clean, redecorated, cheerful house, full of delicious Christmas fare. St John is not satisfied with this answer. He is contemptuous of such 'domestic endearments and household joys' and rather presumptuously informs her that when the two months of 'common place pleasures' are over, he and God will require more of her (pp. 416–17).

Ignoring St John's disapproval, Jane and Hannah get down to work and transform Moor House into a cosy family home, a 'model of bright modest snugness'. Jane shows St John her handiwork, and is both hurt and amazed by his indifference. As she contemplates him reading by the fire, she realizes that he is far more fitted to be a missionary than a husband; this is a very astute observation. He is the sort of man who thrives on hardship and welcomes duty and endurance. It would thus be a 'trying thing to be his wife' and attempt a normal family life.

Diana and Mary are far more appreciative of Jane's hard work and are delighted to be back at Moor House. The three young women have a wonderful time over the Christmas period, relaxing in a mood of 'merry domestic dissipation'. To St John, however, the holiday is irksome, and he is only truly happy when battling through bad weather to visit a needy parishioner.

One morning, St John announces that Rosamond Oliver is engaged to be married, a piece of news which seems to cause him no unhappiness at all. Indeed, he seems almost relieved and more determined than ever to become a missionary.

After the Christmas festivities are over, the family settle to a more regular routine. Jane studies German, Diana peruses encyclopaedias, Mary practises her drawing, and St John attempts to learn Hindustani in preparation for his eastern travels. Jane is aware that St John is studying his sisters and herself, as if comparing them at their work. One afternoon he suddenly asks Jane to give up her German studies and instead help him with his own. He has come to this decision, he says, because out of the three girls Jane appears to be the most assiduous worker (p. 423).

There follow a few tedious months for Jane as she wrestles with St John's grim nature and the difficulties of the language. She has not forgotten Rochester. Her lost love is as painful to her as it has ever been, and although she has inquired of Briggs, and written to Mrs Fairfax, she hears nothing from him or of him. Finally, the full force of her loss comes home to her and she weeps in St John's presence. He is unsympathetic and prescribes a brisk walk with him to make her feel better. They go out and, as they survey the beauty of the moorland, St John asks Jane to come to India with him as his 'helpmate and fellow labourer'. Without actually proposing to her, St John announces that she would make a fine missionary's wife, being 'formed for labour, not for love'. Jane assails St John with doubts. She is not strong enough, she has no vocation, she does not know anything about missionary life. To each of these problems, St John has a well-formulated answer. Jane feels trapped in an 'iron shroud', and begs St John to leave her alone for a short time so that she can think about his proposals. To be a missionary is a challenge which she feels she can rise to. After all, with the terrible loss of Rochester's love, England can bring her little comfort. However, to live as St John's wife is something she knows she could not bear. She realizes that he does not love her, and that she does not love him. Having tasted the joys of requited, if not consummated, love, Jane cannot put up with second best: 'such a martyrdom would be monstrous'.

So, to St John's proposal, she replies that she will go with him to India, but as his sister, not his wife. St John declares that this is impossible. It would appear immoral. Jane replies that it would seem to her immoral to live as a wife to someone whom she did not love. They have reached an impasse. That evening it is obvious to Diana and Mary that Jane and St John have quarrelled. Jane tries to make it up with her cousin, but he is incapable of real reconciliation. The Christian in him accepts her 'faults' but the man cannot show any human warmth.

CHAPTER 35, *pp. 436–45*

St John is still frosty towards Jane. He may have forgiven her for scorning his love, as any good Christian would, but he has not forgotten. Jane is made thoroughly miserable by his behaviour, and continues to seek a reconciliation. However, St John is as grim as ever, and even shows surprise that Jane has not changed her mind. He suggests that if she is really keen to do missionary work, she might travel to India with a married couple he knows. Jane is horrified by this plan. She would have gone with St John, as his sister and fellow labourer, but she has no desire to go to such an inhospitable climate with complete strangers: 'God did not give me my life to throw away,' she declares. Then, thinking of Rochester, she adds that she cannot go to India without first finding out how her beloved is faring (p. 439).

St John is bitterly disappointed with Jane. He had thought her to be one of God's 'chosen'; now she is in mortal danger of becoming a moral castaway. Diana tries to comfort Jane, sharing her cousin's convictions that to marry without love would be 'insupportable – unnatural'. Jane imagines what it would be like to love St John. It would surely be unrequited, for the great man would find no time for such paltry human emotions (p. 441). That night St John reads from Revelation and then intones a prayer for the weak-hearted who might be lured from the paths of goodness by the temptations of the flesh. Jane knows that he is referring to her love for Rochester. She is moved by the texts and their compelling delivery. As she talks with St John that night and he offers her a fortnight to think over his proposals, she is tempted to forget her scruples and give in to this strange, grim, yet commanding man: 'The Impossible – i.e. my marriage with St John – was fast becoming the Possible.' Jane declares that if she truly believed that it was God's will for her to marry St John, she would acquiesce.   .

And it is now that she has an extraordinary experience. She 'hears' Rochester's voice calling out to her in pain and misery (p. 444). Her conviction that it really *is* her loved one, and not a delusion, is so strong that she quite calmly plans to return to Thornfield the next day. She believes that Heaven has indeed shown her her path, and that it leads not to India, but to Thornfield Hall and Rochester's arms.

CHAPTER 36, *pp. 446–54*

When she wakes, Jane finds a note from St John reiterating that she has a fortnight to think over her future, and that he will pray for her soul. Jane ponders alone in her bedroom as the sun rises on a June morning. She is still strongly convinced that it was Rochester calling to her; the experience has 'opened the doors of the soul's cell, and loosened its bands'. Jane explains to Diana and Mary that she must leave to visit friends. They fear for her safety, suspecting where she is in fact going.

On the road to Thornfield, Jane feels like a 'messenger pigeon flying home', and after thirty-six hours of travelling, the pigeon returns to Millcote. She is tempted to ask after Rochester at the local inn. However, she continues towards the Hall, walking through countryside she knows and loves so well. She picks a spot from where she knows she will get a good view of the Hall, then contains her curiosity awhile, dreaming of Thornfield and how it will look to her after her absence.

When she does gaze out across the fields, she sees a terrible sight: Thornfield has been burnt down. It is a blackened ruin. Jane's terrifying dream has come true. She stumbles back to the inn, desperate to find out how the fire was caused and whether Rochester has survived it. The landlord gives the information. Thornfield was burnt down by the mad Mrs Rochester who, in her lunatic frenzy, threw herself down from the battlements and was killed instantly. Her husband was badly injured while escaping and has been left blind. Before this calamity Rochester had apparently been behaving like a lunatic himself, grieving openly for his beloved Jane. He had sent both Adèle and Mrs Fairfax away and had become 'savage in his disappointment', almost 'dangerous'. Now blind and dejected, he is living in Ferndean manor-house, thirty miles away, his only companions being his trusted servant John and his wife Mary. Jane instantly orders a carriage to take her to Ferndean and to Rochester.

CHAPTER 37, *pp. 455–73*

Jane arrives at Ferndean manor. It is a gloomy, dark, forbidding place. As she surveys the house and grounds in the gathering darkness of a cold and windy June evening, she notices a figure emerging from the front door. It is Rochester. He is still strong and even athletic looking, but there is something quite 'desperate and brooding' about his appearance which reminds Jane of some 'wronged and fettered wild beast or bird, dangerous to approach in his sullen woe'. Jane feels a rush of love for this 'sightless Samson', and longs to calm and soothe him. Mary is amazed to see Jane again, and arrangements are made for her to spend the night at Ferndean. Jane asks the parlourmaid to announce that Rochester has a visitor, then, by way of introduction, she takes him his supper tray.

At first Rochester thinks he is only dreaming, relishing a fantasy often indulged since Jane's departure: 'Gentle, soft dream, nestling in my arms now, you will fly, too, as your sisters have all fled before you ...' (p. 459). Jane begins to flesh out the dream, telling Rochester of her new fortune, and promising to be his companion for ever.

How can she bear to be anything else but a mere companion,

Rochester declares, when he must seem quite mutilated and hideous to her. In the fire he lost not only his sight but a hand. He shows her his withered arm. Jane agrees that he has become wild in his appearance, rather like a lion or ragged eagle. Yet she assures him that the pity he invokes in her can only serve to increase her love.

As they eat together, Rochester's mood lightens; he becomes almost joyful, a change indeed from his 'dark, dreary, hopeless life' since Jane left a year ago. That had been a time of 'doing nothing, expecting nothing; merging night in day ... a ceaseless sorrow, and, at times, a very delirium of desire to behold my Jane again' (p. 462). As if to emphasize the reality of her presence, Jane combs Rochester's hair, teasing him and avoiding his questions as to how she has spent the past year.

Next day Jane and Rochester pass the time in the fresh air, sharing confidences. Rochester admits that he would have done anything, sacrificed anything, to have prevented Jane from running away from Thornfield in such destitution. But his jealousies are stirred when she talks about her three cousins, and Rochester realizes that St John is a very eligible bachelor indeed, a 'graceful Apollo' as compared to him, a 'Vulcan – a real blacksmith, brown, broad-shouldered; and blind and lame into the bargain' (p. 466). Jane does not dampen his jealousy; indeed, she wickedly allows Rochester to believe she is engaged to be married to the peerless St John. Then just as the poor Vulcan begins to stamp with rage and hurt, she admits that there is no question of love between her and St John:

All my heart is yours, sir: it belongs to you; and with you it would remain, were fate to exile the rest of me from your presence forever (pp. 468–9).

Moved by her declaration, Rochester proposes marriage. Jane joyfully accepts. As they walk back through the woods together, Rochester recounts an extraordinary experience he had had four days before. He had been in utter despair and had even prayed to God to take his life, so miserable was he without Jane. Almost involuntarily, he had cried out to Jane, and heard, as if in reply, her voice assuring him that she was coming, and then came the words: 'Where are you?' which were accompanied by a cool, mountain wind. It had seemed to

Rochester that their two spirits were meeting, that their souls were magically conversing. Jane realizes that this experience corresponds with her own belief that at the same time she had heard Rochester calling to her across the wild reaches of the night. Rochester gives thanks to God that he has been reunited with Jane, and he asks for strength to enable him to lead a purer life in the future.

CHAPTER 38, *pp. 474–7*

Jane and Rochester are married, quietly and without fuss. Jane writes to her cousins, explaining the circumstances of her marriage.

Ten years pass. Both Diana and Mary have made happy marriages, too, but St John remains a bachelor, devoting the rest of his years to the missionary work he had planned for so long. Adèle is placed in another school so that Jane can be near to visit her, and the little French girl grows up to be a fine young woman: 'A sound English education corrected in great measure her French defects.' Jane and Rochester are blissfully happy and Jane declares:

No woman was ever nearer to her mate than I am: ever more absolutely bone of his bone and flesh of his flesh. I know no weariness of my Edward's society: he knows none of mine ... to be together is for us to be as once as free as in solitude, as gay as in company.

Two years after their marriage Rochester began to discern an improvement in his sight and with the help of a London oculist, his vision was cured to the extent that he no longer needed to be guided and could read and write a little. He was also able to see his first-born son and to see that he had inherited those dark black eyes which had so captivated Jane. The novel ends with St John's prayers to God as he struggles indomitably with his missionary work. He seems to be at peace with his maker and with his fate – as is Rochester, redeemed not just by Jane, his angel of mercy, but through his own suffering.

FORM

What sort of novel is *Jane Eyre*? On the surface it seems to be the autobiography of the heroine written when she is thirty. It moves forward at an exciting pace, but if we examine it carefully we find that Jane only shows us the crucial moments in her life, moments that are central to her main purpose: the story of her love for Rochester and its fulfilment in happy marriage.

As a romantic biography, *Jane Eyre* has similarities with such eighteenth-century novels as Richardson's *Pamela* and *Clarissa*. Like them, it is concerned with the theme of virtue and virtue rewarded. Both Jane and Rochester battle against the faults in their characters and clearly wish to follow the difficult road to virtue. Unlike the eighteenth-century novels, however, Jane's and Rochester's struggles are real, poignant, sometimes funny, and not loaded with sententious sermonizing. Charlotte Brontë gave new life to the 'moral' novel.

Jane Eyre is also an adventure story. It uses one of the novel's oldest traditions – the 'picaresque' or 'travelling' novel – to enhance this. We have seen (p. 11) how important each of Jane's five journeys is. Each is a voyage of the soul as well as the body and portends a shift in dramatic tension. In addition, Charlotte Brontë was also influenced by the 'Gothic' novel, the far-fetched adventure story, full of melodrama and coincidence. The riven chestnut tree, the blood-red moon, the restrained lunatic, supernatural voices in the wind – all were familiar devices popularized in such works as Mrs Anne Radcliffe's *The Mysteries of Udolpho*. In Charlotte Brontë's work they become far truer and more poetic, evocative symbols of her real interest: the psychology of passion. They serve to heighten the drama of this and so stimulate the reader and urge him on.

Thus, in conclusion, we can say that Charlotte Brontë borrowed many of the artificial traditions of her time but gave them the real and poetic force of her genius, creating thereby a novel of compelling force. The childhood scenes at Gateshead, for example, are wonderfully observed, but the scene in the red-room gives them a genuine horror and depth. This is how persecution *feels* to a young child, even if people are rarely so cruel in real life. Jane's and Rochester's love is meaningful to every generation. The storms, blood-red moons, lunatics and fires heighten our excitement, galvanize our interest, so that we feel the full force of the passion. It is through melodrama handled by a poet that we feel the truth of the passion. This accounts for the novel's power.

Characters

JANE EYRE

During the course of the novel we see Jane Eyre develop from a ten-year-old girl living miserably at Gateshead with the Reeds, to a radiantly happy and mature woman of thirty, married to her beloved Mr Rochester. In the course of these twenty years Jane has her share of unhappiness and strife and it is the way in which she battles against hardships that makes her such an admirable heroine: intelligent, gallant and morally strong. We are not told much about the ten years of happy married life with Rochester, apart that is, from the moving description of their love for one another, towards the end of the final chapter (pp. 475–6). It is a fitting conclusion. The reader feels strongly that good has triumphed: goodness being personified in the character of Jane Eyre. However, Jane is no 'goody-goody'. How flabby and dull the novel would be if she were. Her final glorious happiness is hard won and the fight is not always against the world, but against the flaws in her own character.

Pride and a certain intellectual snobbery are Jane's potential vanquishers. When we first see her at Gateshead, mercilessly teased by the abominable Reed children, Jane's only haven is her fierce pride. Described variously by members of the household as a 'rat', 'fury', 'mad cat' and, worst of all, 'liar', Jane's pride and abomination of her relations leave no room for the Christian doctrine of turning the other cheek. She knows the Reeds are her enemies and has not the slightest intention of loving them. She has yet to learn that pride is an admirable characteristic if tempered with gentleness towards others – but this is a lesson to be learned later from Helen Burns.

The self-respect which results from pride in oneself is very different from the savage fighting spirit Jane shows when she avenges herself upon Mrs Reed in chapter 4 (p. 68).

Certainly Jane's petulance and viciousness are understandable, given the extreme provocation and loneliness in which they were nurtured. Nonetheless, Jane learns a valuable lesson after her confrontation with Aunt Reed: that to break another human being's spirit is morally wrong. Jane has found her strength but it is a curiously unsatisfying experience (p. 69). As she realizes such victories are despicable and unworthy, so her 'fierce pleasure' drains away. Yet it is only when she comes under the gentle tutelage of Helen Burns at Lowood School that Jane can fully assimilate why her 'victory' over the pathetic Mrs Reed was so distasteful. In chapter 6 at Lowood School we see Helen being baited and scorned by the unpleasant Miss Scatcherd, and yet submitting meekly. To the savage, angry little Jane Eyre such submission is bewildering: 'When we are struck at without reason, we should strike back again very hard,' reasons Jane. Helen patiently explains that emotional strength in the face of adversity is the doctrine of Christ (p. 90). This is a vital moment in the formation of Jane's character although one feels that it is not just Christ's message which turns a 'bitter and truculent' little girl towards more reasonable behaviour, but also Helen's sensible, personal philosophy: 'Life appears to me too short to be spent nursing animosity, or registering wrongs.' From now on, Jane becomes more detached from the turbulence of her life, its injustices and pains. Indeed, in the following chapter, we see her bravely suffering the indignity of standing upon a stool amidst the Lowood pupils as punishment for being a liar, an accusation made by the odious Mr Brocklehurst. Instead of the rage and hysteria she suffered in the terrible red-room at Gateshead, Jane is calmer and more dignified now. Pride is transmuted to self-respect, and considering the pilgrimages she has yet to undergo, such inner strength is her salvation.

Yet it is the relic of Jane's pride and her stubbornness that so attracts Mr Rochester. Being a proud and strong-minded man himself, Rochester finds it all too easy to trample on other people's feelings, and make them seem foolish. But with Jane, he has found a worthy adversary for his intellectual and emotional sparring. In their conversations we see Jane playfully countering the harsh and ruthless Rochester logic. In chapter 13, Jane and Rochester have their first verbal sparring match, and it is obvious that Rochester is both impressed and amused by his little governess's spirit, recognizing her pride and finding himself attracted to it. He asks whether she has help painting the pictures Adèle shows him: 'No indeed', cries Jane. 'Ah, that pricks pride', counters Rochester.

Through Rochester more of Jane's character is now revealed. We knew that she had been a studious pupil at Lowood and even at Gateshead was a voracious reader (even if reading there was merely an escape from the loneliness of her days). Now, faced with the stern intellect of Mr Rochester, Jane shows she has a keen wit and careful intelligence, which is much appreciated by her master (p. 166). With Rochester, Jane is extremely articulate; one wonders where, incidentally, in the desolation of Gateshead and Lowood, she had the chance to converse with such facility and exchange ideas with such panache. Throughout the novel, Jane's encounters with Rochester uncover a side of her which is almost sophisticated, and certainly shows familiarity with the flirtatious behaviour between man and woman. Look, for example, at how she counters Rochester's fabrication of an impending marriage to Miss Ingram in chapter 19 with her pretence of engagement to St John Rivers in chapter 37. There is a playfulness and inventiveness between the two which enlivens the scenes they share. No wonder Rochester calls Jane his 'provoking puppet', his 'sprite', his 'malicious elf'. Through Rochester's eyes we are aware that Jane, his 'little Janet' is still a girl, yet unlike the girl at Gateshead and Lowood, here is a girl with a sense of humour and the ability to manipulate someone as apparently immovable as Rochester. Look again at chapter 24 when Rochester woos his 'pet' with an excessively silly and sentimental song, only to be rebuffed by the 'pet' with a telling critique of the lyrics. Jane is determined to remain sensible not just because she is so by nature and from experience, but because she has learnt that to keep her distance from Rochester will only serve to intrigue and stimulate him. How worldly she has become (near the end of chapter 24, p. 301):

... this is the best plan I can pursue with you, I'm certain I like you more than I can say but I'll not sink into a bathos of sentiment – and with this needle of repartee I'll keep you from the edge of the gulf, too, and moreover maintain by its pungent aid that distance between you and myself most conducive to our real mutual advantage.

Again through Rochester's eyes we are aware of another of Jane's characteristics: that of disarming honesty. Remember how she fights against the lies and injustices of Gateshead, only ironically to be accused later by Mr Brocklehurst of being a liar. She has not lost her stern regard for the truth; she has now learnt to be relentlessly truthful about herself. Already infatuated by Rochester, she learns in chapter 16 of his possible marriage to Miss Ingram. Horrified by her self-delusion in regarding herself as his special favourite, she makes herself study the truth (p. 190). Jane forces herself to look into the mirror and paint her own portrait, then entitle it as she believes in all truthfulness 'Portrait of a Governess disconnected, poor and plain'. But what first catches Rochester's attention is precisely this very truthfulness, especially her unflattering remarks about his looks (p. 162).

Never having been mothered or flattered herself, Jane is hesitant about being pampered, and, indeed, mightily distrusts it. In chapter 24 we have the amusing spectacle of Jane and Rochester shopping in Millcote, an experience which Jane finds 'somewhat harassing'. She distrusts Rochester's desire to have her 'glittering like a parterre' in silks and satins. And yet, is there not a certain coquettishness behind this quaint disavowal of vanity? Is not Jane determined to be the very opposite of Céline Varens or Blanche Ingram, knowing that Mr Rochester has rejected both?

Boldness in placing herself unadorned before Rochester is a prelude to Jane's great moral and physical bravery in leaving the man she truly loves to tramp across the countryside, bereft of friends and money. In chapter 28 we see Jane reduced to a desperate state; starving, she is forced to beg and since she is without shelter she must sleep on the bare moor. When she is first turned away from the Riverses' cosy hearthside she knows that she is indeed close to death, yet she endeavours to face her suffering with equanimity (p. 361). The rock of this fortitude is her moral decisiveness in not becoming Rochester's mistress, however much she loves him and recognizes the unique power she has to redeem him through her love. Walking away from Rochester into the unknown required great bravery, and this does not minimize the very real and passionate nature of their relationship. Jane's passion for Rochester is not just of an intellectual kind. If it were then Jane's character would be somewhat lacking in humanity. It is obvious from the moment Jane first sees Rochester in chapter 12 that she is attracted to him as a man, and from this moment on she is constantly aware of his physical presence and masculinity. In chapter 17 we see Jane finally admitting to herself that she is deeply in love with Rochester (p. 203). It is a full acknowledgement of this passion which makes Jane so determined to resist the cold and loveless advances of St John.

Jane also has great reserves of sympathy for others throughout the novel, and a wonderful capacity for friendship, both characteristics perfectly in tune with a passionate and intense nature. Jane's first real friendship is with Helen Burns, a friendship which ends in Helen's death (chapter 9), a death much comforted by little Jane's presence: 'And I clasped my arms close around Helen: she seemed dearer to me than ever. I felt as if I could not let her go; I lay with my face hidden on her neck.' Jane's second most important friendship is with St John's sister, Diana. Sympathy for others, however different in nature, is shown in Jane's gentleness towards the frivolous Adèle; gentleness which is certainly more pronounced when in chapter 15 Jane is told of her charge's illegitimacy (p. 176).

Although she does not form a deep friendship with the beautiful and rich Miss Oliver, who would be happy to marry the 'inexorable' St John, Jane is both sympathetic and generous to someone who is so utterly different from her: as attractive and lucky as Jane is plain and unlucky. Jane even allows herself some sympathy for the jilted Miss Ingram – and, towards the Riverses' old retainer, Hannah, who was ready to turn Jane out into the cold to die (chapter 28), Jane is all forgiveness.

It is a long journey that Jane has to make from the sullen little girl at Gateshead to the kind and devoted schoolmistress in Morton, and thence to the loving wife of a blind husband at the novel's close. Yet it is a journey which is entirely believable for the reader. Jane

Eyre is a character study both memorable and unique in English fiction.

ROCHESTER

Of all the characters in *Jane Eyre*, Rochester is the most powerful and the most enigmatic, the most carefully described, yet the most subjectively viewed. It is fair to say that Charlotte Brontë was a little in love with her hero. The reader 'senses' Rochester; he is not a caricature who is easily detached from the novel. You cannot pin him down and dissect him as you can St John, or Mrs Reed, or Brockle-hurst. The man's masculinity and strength pervade the atmosphere of the novel and, like a character in real life, his personality seems infinitely changeable and adaptable. There is something majestic, mysterious, cynical and careworn about him.

If one of the main themes of *Jane Eyre* is the struggle people under-take to conquer the bad side of their characters and follow the thorny path of goodness, then Rochester is a dramatic embodiment of this struggle. He is a man with a past pitted with wrongdoings. And yet he is not bad at heart. He must be judged as a victim of circumstance, swindled and contaminated by lesser mortals whom he has either loved or trusted, and finally brought low by people he despises. At the end of the novel, Jane describes him as a 'sightless Samson' and it is a powerful and accurate image for this brave, decent, virile man, harassed into bad temper and gloom by the savage disappointments of life.

Charlotte Brontë spends a great deal of time and trouble describing the physical appearance of Rochester, and although the power of this description belies a certain fascination the author has for her hero, it is also intended that the reader sense Rochester's virility and magnetism. Remember how St John is portrayed as a rather cold man: 'Had he been a statue instead of a man, he could not have been easier.' Rochester is no perfect model of masculine beauty; indeed, his features are irregular, his hair dark and shaggy, his face often clouded with clashing emotions. But there is no doubt that he is a sexual being, and a passionate man, unlike the ascetic and zealous St John. When we first see Rochester in chapter 12, he is riding recklessly through the countryside near Thornfield. Jane is frightened lest the sound of pounding hooves herald the legendary 'Gytrash'. Although she is relieved to find that both horse and rider appear safely unspectral, the link between man and beast has been skilfully made. When Jane is finally reunited with Rochester at Ferndean (chapter 37) there is still something of the Gytrash about Rochester. Rochester is no 'poor puny' creature (in Blanche's words), 'not fit to stir a step beyond papa's park gates ...' At her first encounter with him, Jane describes Rochester as having a 'considerable breadth of chest ... a dark face, with stern features and a heavy brow'; and later:

... he looked preciously grim, cushioning his massive head against the swelling back of his chair, and receiving the light of the fire on his granite hewn features, and in his great dark eyes; for he had great, dark eyes, and very fine eyes, too – not without a certain change in their depths sometimes, which, if it was not softness, reminded you at least of that feeling.

In chapter 17, Jane compares his 'native pith and genuine power' with the 'grace' and 'languid elegance' of the other guests at Thornfield.

Jane's description of Rochester (p. 204) is of a passionate man. He has felt love, jealousy and hatred; has experienced the 'rocks bristling ... the breakers boil' during his love affair with Céline Varens, Adèle's mother. When Jane declares that she must leave him (ch. 27), he cries out:

Jane, I am not a gentle tempered man – you forget that: I am not long enduring, I am not cool and dispassionate. Out of pity to me and yourself, put your finger on my pulse, feel how it throbs, and – beware!

In chapter 36, the landlord of the inn at Millcote describes Rochester's behaviour after Jane had left him: 'he grew savage – quite savage in his disappointment: he was never a wild man, but he got quite dangerous after he lost her.'

Rochester is indeed not a wild man: he may act wildly or passionately at times, but his heart is ruled by a clear head. He is highly intelligent, and enjoys the company of other intelligent people. One of his most obvious characteristics is a cool contempt for lesser mortals. He does not suffer fools gladly, and cannot bear shams. Thus he is drawn to the intellectual and sincere Jane, and bored and repelled by the shallow and unoriginal Blanche. Jane understands this form of intellectual snobbery, as she shares it to a large degree: in chapter 15 she describes Rochester as:

... proud, sardonic, harsh to inferiority of every description: in my secret soul I knew that his great kindness to me was balanced by an unjust severity to many others.

Yet he is never unjustly severe to those people who, however humble, commend themselves to him by their sincerity and lack of pretensions. He is kind to his servants, settling upon Mrs Fairfax an annuity for life when Jane leaves and he retires to Ferndean. Although the frivolous Adèle reminds him too forcefully at times of her mother, he does not hesitate to adopt her and provide for her. Contempt for stupider, shallower people he may have – Blanche he describes amusingly as an 'extensive armful'; Céline's lover as a 'brainless and vicious youth I ... had never thought of hating because I despised him so absolutely'; Bertha, 'what a pigmy intellect she had – and what great propensities' – but this does not prevent him from acting with decency and courage towards them should the occasion arise. He is the sort of man who may despise people, but would nonetheless risk his life to save theirs. The fire at Thornfield shows Rochester at his most courageous (p. 454).

Rochester also has a humorous, even playful side to his character. He loves sparring intellectually with Jane, and playing upon her innocence. He is excellent company, and with his guests around him the life and soul of the party. His plan to dress up as an old gypsy woman so as to discover both Blanche's and Jane's real feelings about him is inventive, if rather naughty. With little Adèle he can be quite charming, although he teasingly avers that he cannot abide the 'French brat'. He is accomplished, versatile, talented, travelled and sophisticated, yet without his Jane, his 'good angel', he is a lifeless puppet, broken-hearted and bitterly disillusioned by life. Jane provides the key to unlock his soul and illuminate all his good qualities. It is she who can quieten the rumblings of anger in his soul, and transform the maimed lion into perhaps not a meek lamb, but at least a well-tempered eagle.

ST JOHN

The character of St John Rivers is a masterly study in tortured puritanism. His sister Diana describes him as 'inexorable as death', and indeed, the key to his personality is his indomitable will. His life is a permanent struggle against the temptations of the world, and he goes into battle armed with an iron discipline. Look at how he explains his feelings about Rosamond (p. 400). Above all else, St John is ambitious to fulfil his life's vocation as a missionary. Everything else is subservient to this: 'I honour endurance, perseverance, industry, talent; because these are the means by which men achieve great ends, and mount to lofty eminence'. He thus finds it difficult to inhabit the 'frivolous' world, as Eliza Reed describes it, and is repulsed by mediocrity, domesticity, and any form of indulgence. Watching him in his study (ch. 34), Jane comes to the conclusion that it would be a 'trying thing to be his wife', for 'he lived only to aspire – after what was good and great, certainly; but still he would never rest; nor approve of others resting round him'. Scorning the cosy festivities at Christmas, he prepares to battle against the sleet and snow to visit a parishioner in need. And yet, humourless and stern though he be, there is an essential goodness about the man, and a very real sincerity. After all, it is he who literally saves Jane's life and offers her a home and employment. His friendship, which may be devoid of sentimentality, softness and sympathy, is at least true and stalwart. As Jane says of him in the last chapter, he is 'firm, faithful and devoted', someone to admire, but not someone who would be content with the ordinary vicissitudes of human life. His sights are set high, and such ambition is a lonely business. In chapter 34, Jane visualizes this very clearly, and there is no doubt that she admires St John (pp. 418–19). However, she adds that he would be 'at the fireside, too often a cold cumbrous column, gloomy and out of place'. Here we have a truly interesting character study. Charlotte Brontë shows both sides to St John's character: this is no mere caricature of a priggish, cold-hearted parson. The reader cannot help but have affection for him, in the same way that Jane remains loyal and friendly. And it is important to note that it is St John who has the 'last word' in the novel, as we picture him bravely preparing himself for death in the service of God.

HELEN BURNS

It is very difficult to depict a truly good character. Wholeheartedly wicked people always appear interesting in plays and novels because badness is often more dynamic than virtue, especially the rather passive form of virtue we associate with Helen Burns. It is difficult to imagine what Helen would be like were she strong and healthy, for much of her passivity derives from her chronic illness. Perhaps if she were a 'normal' young girl like Jane, she might be more tempted to veer from her chosen path, but as the character appears in the novel any battles with soul, spirit or conscience have ceased. Helen has an unworldly quality about her, a result of an achieved inner peace as much as continuing illness. In chapter 8 (p. 101) she rebukes Jane for dwelling on past slights. It is useful to compare Helen's Christianity with St John's. Both scorn the world, and both are single-minded. Helen's character is the softer and more pliant of the two, however; she is as gentle as St John is stern but both in their own ways offer Jane real friendship.

Helen also has in abundance a quality lacking in St John: patience. She bears the spiteful baiting of Miss Scatcherd with saintly serenity, and accepts her inevitable and lonely death in the same spirit.

Helen's influence upon Jane is profound, and of great importance to the girl's development. Helen's character might seem somewhat insipid and lifeless but insofar as she makes Jane shed her crippling inability to forgive and forget, she plays a vital role.

BERTHA MASON

Bertha, Rochester's first wife, cannot speak for herself in the novel, and it is perhaps one of the weaknesses of the novel that the reader is expected to accept as the only testimonial to her character the descriptions offered by Rochester. The Bertha we see is so far gone in madness as to be more animal than human. In chapter 26, Jane sees the lunatic for the first time (p. 321). She appears to have no sane moments: she is either laughing in the chilling and demonic manner which had first so terrified Jane, or growling like a wild animal and flinging herself upon Mason or Rochester. Her attack on Mason is particularly horrible as she not only stabs but bites him, tearing his flesh with her teeth.

This portrait of the first Mrs Rochester is typical of a Gothic horror novel: Bertha is the 'stock' lunatic, and Charlotte Brontë offers us no insight into why she became mad, or what it felt like to be locked away in the attics of Thornfield. (Interestingly enough, the novelist Jean Rhys was so fascinated by the first Mrs Rochester's predicament that she wrote a novel about her, *Wide Sargasso Sea*.) Some of the insensitivity inherent in Charlotte Brontë's treatment of the mad Mrs Rochester derives from a lack of interest in madness during the nine-teenth century, and an abysmal ignorance about its causes and treat-ment. A modern novelist, brought up on Freud, Jung, and the army of their followers, would attempt a more searching study in character and behaviour. We do know a little about Bertha's early life, however. Rochester tells Jane (ch. 27) that when he first met Bertha she was 'the boast of Spanish Town', 'a fine woman' in the style of Blanche Ingram: tall, dark, majestic. However, he soon discovers that her 'caste of mind' was 'common, low, narrow, and singularly incapable of being led to anything higher, expanded to anything larger'. As madness creeps upon her, these defects flourish. Rochester becomes more and more repelled by her and this repulsion transmits itself forcefully. Unable to bear her 'wolfish cries' any longer, he devises a plan to keep her safely incarcerated at Thornfield while he travels through Europe. The modern reader cannot help but feel sympathy for Bertha, as indeed Jane does, once: 'It is cruel – she cannot help being mad,' she exclaims (ch. 27), but Charlotte Brontë intends us to forgive Rochester his 'vindictive antipathy' on account of his wife's previous character.

GRACE POOLE

Grace is a shadowy figure and, for two-thirds of the book, her identity is doubtful. Like Jane, the reader is intended to assume that Grace is the Thornfield lunatic, prone to burning people in their beds and laughing in a demonic fashion. Yet from the first, the reader, like Jane, cannot quite equate the stolid Grace with such horrors. When Jane first hears 'preternatural' laughter echo through the corridors of Thornfield, Mrs Fairfax implies that Grace is the culprit, but Jane admits to herself that 'any apparition less romantic, or less ghostly could scarcely be conceived'. Grace is 'between thirty or forty; a set, square made figure, red-haired, and with a hard plain face'. After she saves Rochester from his burning bedroom, Jane comes near to confronting Grace the next morning (ch. 16). However, she is again amazed at the difference between Grace the supposed mad woman, terrible in her passion, and Grace the phlegmatic maid, engaged for her competence with the needle. Indeed, apart from her obvious weakness for drink, Grace is almost a Quakerish character, whose patience and even temper make her an ideal warden for a mad woman; which is what, in chapter 26, we eventually learn she is.

MRS FAIRFAX

Mrs Fairfax, although distantly related to Rochester, works as his housekeeper at Thornfield Hall. When Jane first meets her (ch. 11), she describes the little elderly lady as the 'beau ideal of domestic comfort'. She is kindly and long-suffering, and Jane soon develops a great fondness for her. However, in chapter 12 we sense that Jane finds her company just a trifle boring: 'Mrs Fairfax turned out to be what she appeared, a placid-tempered, kind-natured woman, of competent education and average intelligence' – but not stimulating enough for the young woman who dreams of change and excitement. Mrs Fairfax is the embodiment of cosy mediocrity. Thus she is horrified when Rochester proposes to marry Jane. Such events threaten to unbalance the equilibrium of life as she knows it. She also has more common sense than Jane and, from her experience of the world, 'Gentlemen in his [Rochester's] station are not accustomed to marry their governesses'. We see very little of Mrs Fairfax after chapter 24, although we learn that after the fire at Thornfield, Rochester settles a pension upon her, and she leaves to stay with friends.

MASON

Jane takes an instant dislike to Mason, when he appears at Thornfield (ch. 18). Although the other ladies of the party pronounce him to be 'a love of a creature', a 'beautiful man', the 'ideal of the charming', Jane finds his handsome face rather repellent (p. 219): 'His features were regular, but too relaxed; his eye was large and well cut, but the life looking out of it was a tame, vacant life'. She compares him to Rochester:

The contrast could not be much greater than between a sleek gander and a fierce falcon: between a meek sheep and the rough-coated, keen-eyed dog, its guardian.

Towards Rochester, Mason behaves with deference, almost fear, yet so weak-minded is he that he makes no attempts to stop Briggs interrupting Jane's and Rochester's marriage, although of all people he must have known what torments his brother-in-law had undergone. Rochester pronounces later that he 'cannot hate' the vacillating Mason, because he at least has some 'grains of affection in his feeble mind'.

ADÈLE

Adèle Varens is a young Rosamond Oliver: charming, frivolous, not particularly intelligent, but nevertheless harmless and guileless. When we first meet her she is about eight years old, and speaks an attractive mix of French and English. Jane cannot help but like her, and soon irons out any wayward or spoiled tendencies.

Like her mother, Céline, Adèle adores parties, company and clothes. She prattles and gossips in a superficial way which Jane finds 'hardly congenial to an English mind', yet her gaiety is rather touching; when Jane and Adèle are invited to meet Rochester's guests (ch. 17), she begs Jane to let her pin a flower to her sash. Jane admits that there is something 'ludicrous as well as painful in the little Parisienne's earnest and innate devotion to matters of dress'. However, we learn that Adèle does not turn into a mirror-image of her dissipated mother. When Jane marries Rochester, she puts Adèle into a nearby school in which 'a sound English education corrected in great measure her French defects', and Adèle becomes a 'pleasing and obliging companion: docile, good-tempered, and well-principled'.

BLANCHE INGRAM

Of all the characters in *Jane Eyre*, Blanche is one of the most unpleasant. Charlotte Brontë shows us none of the woman's good points. Thus the portrait is more of a caricature than a well-rounded study; but however one-dimensional she may be, Blanche is truly memorable.

Her physical appearance is important, as she is a woman who sets great store by appearance: as Jane remarks (ch.18) 'she was very showy, but she was not genuine'. Mrs Fairfax describes her magnificent appearance (two-thirds of the way through the chapter, p. 189):

Tall, fine bust, sloping shoulders; long graceful neck, olive complexion, dark and clear noble features; eyes rather like Mr Rochester's, large and black, and as brilliant as her jewels. And then she had such a fine head of hair, raven black . . .

Poor Jane discovers that Blanche is just as splendid in reality, but looking at her more closely sees in her face an all-consuming pride. Rochester is aware of this haughtiness too, and in chapter 24 delivers his judgement upon her: 'Her feelings are concentrated in one – pride'. It is pride which robs Blanche of charm or of any sympathy for others. To Adèle she is cold and dismissive, as Jane notices (p. 215). To Jane she is contemptuous and, as she admits (ch. 17), her contempt extends to all governesses. She relates how she had baited her own governesses, and the descriptions of these cruel persecutions are chilling. We conclude that Blanche's only possible 'virtues' are those which have been carefully cultivated to captivate society: good looks, amusing conversation, wit and vivacity. But as Jane observes (ch. 18), 'her mind was poor, her heart barren by nature: nothing bloomed spontaneously on that soil'.

ELIZA and GEORGIANA REED

Eliza and Georgiana offer a fascinating contrast. Both girls are repellent in their own ways, and as children certainly behaved with heartless cruelty towards Jane. They do not offer to protect her against their brutal brother, and quite simply treat her as if she were a servant, or worse. It is only later (chs. 21 and 22) that we learn more about the two girls and see how their characters have developed in such entirely different ways. They look very dissimilar: Eliza is as thin and puritanical as Georgiana is plump, stylish and frivolous. Jane notices that Eliza has invented for herself an exacting routine, more suited to the ascetic than to a young woman of leisure (three-quarters of the way through chapter 21, p. 263):

She seemed to want no company: no conversation. I believe she was happy in her way: this routine sufficed for her and nothing annoyed her so much as the occurrence of any incident which forced her to vary its clockwork regularity.

Georgiana, on the other hand, spends her time indolently slouching about the house, moaning about the dullness of life at Gateshead, and dreaming of 'past gaiety', and 'dissipations to come'. If anything she cares even less for her sick mother than Eliza does; her head is full of indulgence and nonsense: so full as to allow no room for pity, genuine love or lasting affection. Eliza despises her sister, not for her lack of feeling, but for her uselessness (p. 264). Eliza is also totally uninterested in other people, yet ironically becomes a nun, and eventually Mother Superior, in a French order. Georgiana desperately needs people to entertain and support her, yet cares little for anyone else's misfortunes. Both girls are abominably selfish in different ways: 'one intolerably acrid, the other despicably savourless for the want of it', as Jane astutely remarks.

JOHN REED

John is Mrs Reed's 'darling' son, and when we first see him at Gateshead, a more nasty 14-year-old boy could not be imagined. Jane describes him (middle of chapter 1, p. 41) as

large and stout for his age, with a dingy and unwholesome skin; thick lineaments in a spacious visage, heavy limbs and large extremities. He gorged himself habitually at table which made him bilious, and gave him a dim and bleared eye and flabby cheeks.

As well as teasing and torturing Jane unmercifully, he

twisted the necks of the pigeons, killed the little peachicks, set the dogs at the sheep, stripped the hothouse vines of their fruit, and broke the buds of the choicest plants in the conservatory.

He was rude to his mother, and later in life, when plagued by debts, and senseless with depravity, he never ceases to swindle more and more money out of the wretched woman, whose pathetic inability to check her wayward son does much to bring about his eventual disgrace and suicide.

MRS REED

Unlike the unpleasant Blanche Ingram or the hateful Reverend Brocklehurst, Mrs Reed is not painted in one dimension. Hers is an enthralling study in spite, but a study which allows the character a weaker side. All Mrs Reed's spite is directed towards Jane, but there is no doubt that she experiences some guilt over the treatment she metes out to her niece. Why else should she ask for Jane at her death bed?

When we first encounter Mrs Reed she openly prefers her own children to her niece, will hear nothing against Eliza, Georgiana and John, and gains sadistic satisfaction from punishing Jane for her own children's wrongdoing. Later we learn that this aversion to Jane derives from her late husband's obvious preference for the little orphan to his own children. Mrs Reed had been small-minded, insecure and stupid enough to feel jealous of a baby, and she is too proud to admit this jealousy and attempts to hide it. When Jane rounds upon her (ch. 4), 'People think you are a good woman, but you are bad; hard hearted ...', the proud veneer cracks. Mrs Reed is quickly reduced to a trembling shadow of her former self; the 'peculiar eye which nothing could melt; and the somewhat raised, imperious, despotic eyebrow' are revealed to Jane as components of a mask to hide the woman's inner turmoil. When Jane returns to Gateshead years later to pay her last respects to Mrs Reed, she finds a truly pathetic woman. Her daughters feel nothing for her, and her son has swindled and cheated her. She is now haunted by her hatred for Jane, a hatred which has grown out of all proportion and blotted out hope of a guilt-free old age: '... what we think little of in health, burdens us at such an hour as the present is to me'. Yet even when she admits to receiving the letter from Jane's uncle in Madeira, she cannot bring herself to accept Jane's forgiveness and friendship (end of chapter 21, p. 262):

> Poor suffering woman! it was too late for her to make now the effort to change her habitual frame of mind: living, she had ever hated me – dying, she must hate me still.

And so Mrs Reed's death leaves the reader, like Jane, in a 'sombre, tearless dismay'. She has been a tragic figure: hardened by foolish pride, embittered by hatred, yet riddled with guilt.

MISS SCATCHERD

Miss Scatcherd is the despotic history teacher who makes Helen Burns's life all but intolerable at Lowood. We never learn why she singles out Helen, but her treatment is unjust and harsh. Helen bears this treatment with grace, and even explains to Jane that her punishments are often deserved, owing to her inability to be systematic; something that would provoke Miss Scatcherd who is 'naturally neat, punctual and particular'. All Helen will say in defence of herself is that the nagging teacher is 'hasty'. Jane is more apt to condemn Miss Scatcherd as a mean-minded bully:

> ... such spots there are on the disc of the meanest planet; and eyes like Miss Scatcherd's can only see those minute defects, and are blind to the full brightness of the orb (ch. 7).

ROSAMOND OLIVER

Rosamond is a charming cameo; she is as good-looking, in a different way, as Blanche, but far more pleasant. (It is interesting to note, however, that Jane paints both their portraits.) Rosamond, we learn, is an example of 'perfect beauty' (p. 389). We also learn that she is extremely rich and, although she prefers St John Rivers, is not short of eligible suitors. Yet she is not spoilt (p. 394). But Jane adds that she was in the end 'not profoundly interesting or thoroughly impressive', and for these reasons, as well as deducing that she would probably make an unsuitable missionary's wife, St John ignores her, and Rosamond quickly finds someone else to marry, as St John prophesied she would. Seen through the eyes of Jane and St John, poor Rosamond seems rather shallow, yet the image of her girlish beauty and gaiety adds an attractive element to the novel, and also proves that Jane has grown sufficiently secure in herself not to be unduly threatened by the girl's beauty, luck and wealth.

HANNAH

Hannah is a marvellous portrait of the 'honest but inflexible servant' whose devotion to the family she looks after takes precedence over all else. She is a countrywoman and speaks with a thick dialect. She has a natural suspicion of strangers (hence her brusque treatment of Jane when she begs at the door of Marsh End) and a fiercely protective spirit towards her 'charges', Mary, St John and Diana Rivers: 'I thought mo o'th'childer nor of myself: poor things. They've like nobody to tak' care on 'em but me. I'm like to look sharpish.' She is also a great talker, and soon acquaints Jane with the Riverses' family history. One sees Hannah as a jolly, bustling, gossipy type, no great intellect, but good-hearted and full of country lore.

BROCKLEHURST

Brocklehurst is a caricature of hypocrisy, depicted in the vigorous, clear-cut way often associated with Dickens's characters. His physical appearance is awesome. When Jane first sees him she describes him as a 'black pillar'; 'straight, narrow, sable clad shape ... the grim face at the top was like a carved mask'. Mr Brocklehurst is the 'fire and brimstone' type of Christian who delights in stories of infants whose untimely deaths are alleviated by their undoubted piety, yet spares no pity for children whose heavenly admission may be in question. Indeed, he seems to delight in the imagined spectacle of these unfortunates burning in an everlasting fire. Brocklehurst maintains he abhors pride and vanity, yet when we see him for the second time at Lowood, he is accompanied by his family, whose dress and demeanour is anything but humble: 'they were splendidly attired in velvet, silk and furs'. Obviously his own well-being, and the comfort of his family, does not prevent Brocklehurst from sternly pursuing his 'mission' at Lowood.

His hypocrisy is so monstrous that it blinds him to the terrible destruction that bad diet and comfortless accommodation are to wreak upon the Lowood girls. Many of the typhus victims would have survived had it not been for Brocklehurst's parsimony. His 'Christianity' is of the most dangerous kind.

MISS TEMPLE

Miss Temple's kindness, serenity and justice provide the only real ray of hope at Lowood School. Although the principal, she is powerless to change the basic policies of the school, or to persuade Brocklehurst to be more generous. However, she does her utmost to bring some happiness and comfort into her pupils' lives. Thus she allows Jane the 'right of reply' when she is accused by Brocklehurst of being a liar. In the same spirit she arranges a special bread and cheese lunch after the burnt porridge episode. Her kindness to Helen is very special, however. A highly intelligent and sensitive woman herself, she obviously enjoys the company of her enthusiastic and articulate pupil. She also feels a strong maternal love for Helen, and makes her last weeks more comfortable and companionable. After Helen's death, she extends her love to Jane (beginning of chapter 10, p. 116):

... to her instruction I owed the best part of my acquirements; her friendship and society had been my continual solace; she stood me in the stead of mother, governess, and latterly, companion.

When Miss Temple leaves Lowood to marry a clergyman ('almost worthy of such a wife') Lowood is no longer the same for Jane, but when she thinks of leaving she acknowledges a great debt to her principal:

I had imbibed from her something of her nature and much of her habits; more harmonious thoughts; what seemed better regulated feelings had become the inmates of my mind.

BESSIE

Bessie, when we first encounter her, is nursemaid to the Reed children and Jane. She shares the household's partiality for Eliza, John and Georgiana, and is often brusque and thoughtless towards Jane. Yet Bessie's natural good nature and humour make her the only approachable person in the unhappy house and for want of anyone else Jane is naturally drawn to her. Bessie is obviously drawn to Jane, too, and feels pity for the 'little roving, solitary thing' in her charge. Thus she bestows some kindness upon Jane, but Jane barely trusts her because of her 'capricious and hasty temper, and indifferent ideas of principle and justice'.

We meet Bessie twice more after Jane leaves Gateshead: when she unexpectedly appears at Lowood to wish Jane well and find out how she has developed over the eight years since leaving the Reeds; and finally back at Gateshead when Jane returns to see Mrs Reed. Bessie has married, has children and, as Jane observes, has retained her sprightly good looks, quick temper, and insatiable appetite for gossip, which has at least made her astute about the people at Gateshead: '... you will get on whether your relations notice you or not', she says of Jane.

DIANA and MARY RIVERS

Both sisters are gentle and educated girls, devoted to each other and
to their brother, and yet willingly extend love and charity to Jane
when she comes, a complete stranger, into their lives. We learn that
they both adore the countryside as much as their studies, and for
both have an unaffected enthusiasm. Of the two, Diana emerges as
the more forceful and interesting. Jane is particularly drawn to her:
'Our natures dovetailed: mutual affection – of the strongest kind –
was the result'. She has a certain vivacity and an amusing turn of
phrase. When she learns that her brother has plans to transport Jane
off to India for missionary work, she exclaims: 'You are much too
pretty, as well as too good, to be grilled alive in Calcutta!' At the
end of the novel, we learn that Diana has made a happy marriage,
not to a clergyman, but to a 'gallant officer' in the navy, whose exciting
life would undoubtedly suit his wife's liveliness and spirit. Mary
marries the clergyman, a Mr Wharton, who makes her as happy as
her sister.

Commentary

THE LOVE OF JANE AND ROCHESTER

The major theme of *Jane Eyre* is the love between Jane and Rochester. The development of this love, and its final happy consummation, holds the reader's attention from the minute Jane and her master meet (ch. 12), to the novel's conclusion, and Jane's moving testimonial to her marriage (pp. 475–6).

The union between Jane and Rochester is a very real and believable one. Jane falls in love gradually and naturally; Rochester, possibly because he is so much older and more experienced, and in some ways more desperate, claims that he fell for Jane at first sight (p. 339), but admits (at the end of his long, unbroken confession, p. 341) that there came a time when:

> I was now too fond of you ... and when I stretched my hand out cordially, such bloom and light and bliss rose to your young, wistful features, I had much ado often to avoid straining you then and there to my heart.

Jane realizes that she has fallen in love with Rochester (ch. 17) when she sees him for the first time in the company of Blanche and the other guests at Thornfield (p. 203). Throughout the evening she cannot take her eyes from Rochester: she loves his looks, his voice, his easy sociable manner, his 'energy, decision, will'. He may not be a text-book example of male attractiveness, but to Jane her master's features 'were more than beautiful'. She also feels, as all lovers do, that the object of her adoration can see as clearly into her soul, as she can into his. There is real passion in the declaration of her feelings for Rochester (p. 204). Jane always makes it clear that her love for

Rochester is as physical as it is spiritual: a passion of the heart and brain; of the flesh and soul. So intense is their passion for one another that it is entirely possible that they do communicate subliminally (ch. 35), and sense each other calling through the night: Rochester begging Jane to come to him; Jane replying that she is on her way. To Jane this experience was 'like an earthquake': 'it had opened the doors of the soul's cell, and loosed its bands – it had wakened it out of its sleep . . .'. This is the full realization of her love for Rochester, and it is a love so deep and so consuming, that it breaks down the barriers of age, class, wealth, even time and space.

For Rochester, Jane's love is an urgent requirement. Without its redeeming qualities he is a spent force, a 'sightless Samson', 'savage is his disappointment'. At last he has found someone he can truly love and admire and who can, by her good qualities, undo the wrongs and miseries he has experienced through his life. Rochester imbues Jane with supernatural qualities from the beginning of their relationship. She is his 'sprite', 'elf', 'fairy', but most important his 'good angel'. She is the means by which he will become a better, purer, happier person. This redemption through love is a major theme.

Although Jane loves Rochester very much she is not so completely dependent upon his love. Her own self-respect, reverence for a moral code, and love of God are more important to her, and thus she cannot become Rochester's mistress. It is only when Bertha is dead and Rochester truly repents of his past misdemeanours and his attempts to force Jane into a bigamous marriage, that he is 'allowed' his reward. When Jane meets him at Ferndean, he explains how he has come to terms with God (end of chapter 37, p. 471):

I began to see and acknowledge the hand of God in my doom. I began to experience remorse, repentance; the wish for reconciliation to my Maker. I began sometimes to pray: very brief prayers they were, but very sincere.

Their love for one another is now no longer idolatrous or immoral, and Jane and Rochester are at last permitted peace and happiness.

CHRISTIAN VALUES

Another important theme in *Jane Eyre* is the exploration of Christian values. We have seen how Rochester has to expiate his sins and humble himself in front of God before he can have his 'good angel' by his side. Jane, too, has to come to terms with God. When infatuated with Rochester and so bound up with him that she cannot think of anything else, she admits that 'I could not, in those days, see God for his creature: of whom I had made an idol'. She knows that it is morally wrong to become Rochester's mistress and is 'visited' by a heavenly being on the night of her wedding, pleading with her to flee temptation. On the moorland near Whitcross she puts herself into the hands of God, and indeed prays to Him to look after Rochester. In her darkest hours, Jane now attempts to communicate directly with God; thoughts of worldly pleasures no longer blot out His image from her mind. Yet, when tempted to become St John's wife, she knows that Rochester's need for her, of which she learns by paranormal means, is now sanctioned by God: 'I seemed to penetrate very near a Mighty Spirit; and my soul rushed out in gratitude at His feet.' Jane's God is different from St John's. She experiences Him in a mystical, unconventional way.

St John's Christianity is of the sternest kind. He has decided to 'fight the good fight' in the only way he knows how: total self-sacrifice and subservience to a Higher Will. His austerity is daunting, however, and his ambitions to spread the gospel and be a warrior for the Church fit him far more for missionary work than the job of a local parson in a sleepy English village: 'Literally, he lived only to aspire – after what was good and great . . .', Jane says of him (ch. 34), and in the next chapter (middle, p. 441) explains:

> He is a good and great man: but he forgets, pitilessly, the feelings and claims of little people, in pursuing his own large views. It is better, therefore, for the insignificant to keep out of his way; lest in his progress, he should trample them down.

As he had promised, St John eventually goes to India to fulfil his ambitions, and Jane says of him in the last page of chapter 25, (p. 477):

A more resolute and indefatigable pioneer never wrought amidst rocks and dangers. Firm, faithful and devoted, full of energy and zeal, and truth, he labours for his race . . .

There is no doubt that St John's Christianity is of the most sincere kind, unlike Brocklehurst and Eliza Reed who both profess to be followers of Christ but are both in their own ways exceptionally hypocritical. Brocklehurst's Christianity is all bombast and show. He forces the poor half-starved girls from Lowood to walk miles along a cold, unsheltered road to hear him preach the gospel, yet he cares nothing for their comfort or well-being. Eliza chooses to become a nun simply because the well-regulated life of the nunnery suits her solitary and selfish nature. She feels no real charity or love for others; indeed she is relieved to cut off all communication with her sister Georgiana, having previously spitefully ruined a prospective match between Georgiana and an eligible young man.

Helen Burns's Christianity is almost saint-like. She follows the words of Christ to the letter and practises their teachings in her own life. When baited by Miss Scatcherd she turns the other cheek. Helen has the gift of love. St John, sincere, brave and diligent though he may be, has to work hard at loving, and finds patience and grace under stress difficult to achieve. Jane makes the distinction very astutely (ch. 29) when she compares St John's 'evangelical charity' with his sisters', 'spontaneous, genuine, genial, compassion'.

APPEARANCE AND REALITY

The sincerity of people's Christian beliefs in *Jane Eyre* is woven into a larger theme: that of the difference between appearance and reality. Charlotte Brontë is very interested in describing people's physical appearances and contrasting that with their characters. Thus, Blanche is a beauty, although her nature is proud and selfish. Mason is described by the women at Thornfield as being extremely handsome, yet Jane sees behind the mask a pathetic and spineless emptiness. Georgiana Reed is preferred to Jane at Gateshead because she is so adorable to look at: 'I dote on Miss Georgiana', exclaims Miss Abbot, one of the maids: 'Little darling! – with her long curls and her blue eyes, and such a sweet colour as she has.' Jane realizes that if she were more attractive, her time at Gateshead would have been easier: 'I know that had I been a sanguine, brilliant, careless, exacting, handsome, romping child – though equally dependent and friendless – Mrs Reed would have endured my presence more complacently'. Jane is well aware of her own plainness and to drive home the point forces herself to paint a self-portrait: 'Portrait of a Governess: disconnected, poor and plain'. She is also aware of Mr Rochester's physical irregularities, and indeed, in answer to his question, 'do you think me handsome?', can only reply, in all truthfulness, that he is not. She is able to see behind the 'mask' of human beauty, and is only really interested in the human soul behind. Thus, she mistrusts Rochester's desire to have her dressed in silks and satins when she becomes his wife (beginning of chapter 24, p. 288):

And then you won't know me, sir, and I shall not be your Jane Eyre any longer, but an ape in an harlequin's jacket – a jay in borrowed plumes. I would as soon see you, Mr Rochester, tricked out in stage-trapping as myself clad in a court-lady's robe; and I don't call you handsome, sir, though I love you most dearly; far too dearly to flatter you. Don't flatter me.

Jane could not bear to be Rochester's quasi-wife, either, when he proposes to make her his mistress. Such an arrangement will not tally with her sense of sincerity and truthfulness. Eventually he is forced to accept this (near the end of chapter 27, p. 345):

Conqueror I might be of the house; but the inmate would escape to heaven before I could call myself possessor of its clay dwelling place.

Jane knows that to live in luxury and sensual bliss as Rochester's mistress is a delightful temptation but that the reality would entail suffering and guilt on her part. It would be an existence akin to the sort of charade she has watched Blanche and Rochester play: a show, a performance, hiding lies and deceit. Jane believes that she has been privy to the 'real' Rochester. She sees into his soul from very early on. When she declares her love for him (middle of chapter 23, p. 281), she exclaims:

I am not talking to you now through the medium of custom, conventionalities, or even of mortal flesh: it is my spirit that addresses your spirit; just as if both had passed through the grave, and we stood at God's feet, equal – as we are.

Unsure whether his proposal of marriage is genuine, Jane studies his face in the moonlight, trying to discern the workings of his mind. And when they are finally reunited, Rochester's physical appearance – his withered arm and sightless eyes – do not offend or discourage Jane. She knows and loves the man underneath.

The mystery of Thornfield is woven into the theme of appearance versus reality. To Jane, Thornfield Hall is a charming place. To Rochester it is a 'mere dungeon'. 'The glamour of inexperience is over your eyes', he explains to Jane,

and you can see it through a charmed medium: you cannot discern that the gilding is slime and the silk draperies cobwebs, that the marble is sordid slate, and the polished woods mere refuse chips and scaly bark.

To Jane, kept deliberately in the dark, it is Grace Poole who is the dangerous lunatic. The reality is too terrible for Rochester to admit. The wife he has incarcerated in the attics of Thornfield is the real lunatic, yet she can hardly be said to be his true wife. Jane glimpses the truth through dreams and extrasensory experiences. The storm in the garden on the evening of Rochester's proposal is a warning that all is not well, that behind the façade of happiness lies the reality of suffering. Her dreams of Rochester disappearing out of her sight as she watches from the roof of Thornfield, and then the sight of a ghastly, ruined, burnt-out house, are intimations of the real nature of her hopes and dreams which when finally dashed, appear like a charade or a miasma: 'A Christmas frost had come at midsummer: a white December storm had whirled over June; ice glaced the ripe apples, drifts crushed the blowing roses ...' There is nothing more bitter than the discovery that all is not what it seems, and Jane is heartbroken to discover the truth about Rochester's first marriage – as heartbroken as she had been when, years before, she had been unjustly called a liar by Mrs Reed. Truth is very dear to Jane, and her life is a struggle to disentangle truth from reality. She is not interested in the glitter and show of superficial existence, but in the real meaning of life. Her struggle to find truth is mirrored by the struggles and vicissitudes of other characters: Rochester, St John and Helen.

RIGHTEOUSNESS

The theme of the human soul struggling to find righteousness and eventual peace is an echo of Bunyan's *Pilgrim's Progress* in which Everyman makes his way through the world and all its troubles, encountering temptation on the way, yet managing to stick to the winding and thorny path of goodness. Jane's struggles with her soul are heartrending and she makes a great personal sacrifice when she leaves Rochester. She is not simply tempted by his love, but she is also tortured by the knowledge that he needs her very desperately. She is his redemption, his reward, the means by which he can rectify past sins and lead a purer, happier, more God-fearing life in the future. Jane explains her despair and her terrible predicament to the reader (end of chapter 27, p. 348):

May you never appeal to Heaven in prayers so hopeless and so agonized as in that hour left my lips: for never may you, like me, dread to be the instrument of evil to what you wholly love.

Her suffering and struggles are dramatically played out in the next few days. By following what she knows to be the lonely path of goodness, Jane has ostracized herself from society: she is turned away as she begs at doorways; she is regarded with contempt and suspicion; and she is subject to the inhospitable nature of the countryside. Like King Lear battling against the storm in Shakespeare's play, a storm which symbolizes the cruelty of man, so Jane's sojourn on the cold and wet moors symbolizes her hard choice, a choice which has made her turn her back upon the delights of sensual and spiritual love, luxury, sunshine, companionship, intellectual stimulation and forced her to wander the bleak countryside alone and utterly dejected. Her only comfort is the conviction that what she is doing is right, and that although she may remain unhappy and unloved for the rest of her life, she will at least be at peace with herself. Later, when she is the schoolmistress at Morton, she asks herself whether she made the right decision; whether she should have given in to temptation and forfeited the struggle (beginning of chapter 31, p. 386):

Which is better? – To have surrendered to temptation; listened to passion; made no painful effort – no struggle – but to have sunk down in the silken snare ... Whether it is better, I ask, to be a slave in a fool's paradise in Marseilles – fevered with delusive bliss one hour – suffocating with the bitterest tears of remorse and shame for the next – or to be a village schoolmistress, free and honest, in a breezy mountain nook in the healthy heart of England?

St John has to make a terribly difficult choice, too, between his love for Rosamond, and his vocation as a missionary. He is perhaps made of sterner stuff than Jane, but there is no doubt that his fantasies of life with Rosamond are very tempting indeed (near the end of chapter 32, p. 399):

Fancy me yielding and melting, as I am doing: human love rising like a freshly opened fountain in my mind and overflowing with sweet inundation all the field I have so carefully and with such labour prepared ...

But nothing must stand in the way of St John's struggle, and for a man so keen to conquer the temptations of the flesh, the hard life of a missionary 'amidst rocks and dangers' suits him well. In India, his toils take on a majestic, exciting, and deeply-satisfying symbolism.

Jane and Rochester are content to remain in the confines of domestic bliss; their struggle has been to find each other and be worthy of each other. Rochester has at last submitted to God, and allowed his pride to be melted by the tears of remorse: 'I was forced to pass through the valley of the shadow of death', Rochester explains to Jane (ch. 37) when he describes the miseries he underwent, pining for his lost love. Yet through his suffering he learns humility. Before Jane he prays to God to forgive him his past immoralities: 'I humbly entreat my Redeemer to give me strength to lead henceforth a purer life than I have done hitherto!'

It was the patient and saintly Helen who taught Jane patience and humility and that to fight tooth and nail against slights, real or supposed, was wrong. Both Jane and Rochester, through the vicissitudes of life, accept humility and, unlike St John whose struggles with life need to be undertaken on a lofty plain, they make use of what they have learnt in their darkest hours to build a lifetime of love and companionship. Their reward is each other; Helen and St John seek a heavenly reward and do not expect to taste earthly joys. For Jane and Rochester, the culmination of their struggles and sufferings is a wonderfully happy union of mind and body, sanctioned by God. They are each other's just reward.

Glossary

Aërial lace: ethereal, dainty lace

Agate: in mind

Albion: Greek and Roman name for Britain

Alpha and Omega: the first and last letters of the Greek alphabet; together they mean the beginning and the end

Apollo Belvedere: Apollo was the Sun God of Greek mythology and supposedly very beautiful. The Belvedere statue of the God is in the Vatican in Rome

Apothecary: druggist, chemist, and often the local doctor as well

Ariel: Prospero's servant in *The Tempest* who was half-human, half-spirit, and who could perform magical tricks and command the natural elements

Auditress: listener

August: majestic, venerable

Babel: biblical reference to a tower built by people of different races speaking different languages which resulted in terrible confusion. Has come to mean a noisy confusion

Bairn: little child

Barmecide: imaginary, deriving from a character in the Arabian Nights

Beau ideal: embodiment

Beck: stream

Beldame: old woman or hag

Beulah: a promised land, referred to in Isaiah

Black-avised: badly thought of

Blades: like sparks, young gallants

Blent: mingled

Blond: silken lace

Bohemian glass: Bohemia is now Czechoslovakia, and is still famous for beautiful glass

Bombazeen: black woollen or silk or cotton fabric, often worn for mourning

Boon of a brand snatched from the burning: the great gift of a person who has been saved from damnation

Boots: luggage holders

Boudoir: a lady's private room

Brackish: half saltwater, half freshwater

Brahma: Hindu God

Brake: thicket

Bridewell: notorious London prison

Bronze scrag: probably referring to Rochester's bronzed neck

Brown stuff frocks: dresses made from brown material

Brownie: benevolent domestic goblin

Cachinnation: loud laughter

Cairngorm: mountainous and bleak part of Scotland, famous for semi-precious stones

Cameo head: tiny framed portrait

Cant: jargon

Canzonette: short song, quite like a madrigal

Carthage: North African city famous for its great general Hannibal, who inflicted many defeats upon the Roman Empire

Cast: condition, type

Caste: class

Cavillers: people who raise tricky and argumentative questions

Charades: party game in which each team acts out a word or phrase in several scenes

Charivari: medley of sounds

Chemises: blouses

Chicken in the pip: the 'pip' is a disease which affects poultry

Chidden: told off

Chimeras: daydreams, forebodings

Coadjutor: assistant, in a religious sense

Collect: short prayer

Con spirito: with spirit

Conning: studying by learning something by heart

Consumption: disease of the lungs also called tuberculosis

Corsair song: pirate song

Crabbed: intricate

Crape: gauze-like material with wrinkled surface worn for mourning

Creole: descendant of Negro settlers in the West Indies

Curl paper: curler made from paper

Cuyp: Dutch landscape painter

Cynosure: centre of attraction

Danaë: mother of Perseus

Dandy valet: smart manservant

Demas: a minor character in John Bunyan's *Pilgrim's Progress*

Dentelles: combs

Diademed: crowned

Dian: the Goddess Diana, goddess of chastity and hunting

Dished: jilted

Divers: several

Dives: The rich man in St Luke's gospel, who is sent to hell, not for having been wealthy, but for ignoring the beggar Lazarus who starved at his gates

Dowagers: widows with property

Dudgeon: resentment

Dun and sere: dull and withered

DV: Deo volente, God willing

Eastern Emir: Arab prince

Ebon: black

Effluvia: smell, sense of

Elastic: flexible, adaptable

Eld: age

Electric travail: lightning

Entailed: it had been decided how the estate would be divided up

Eulogiums: praises

Eutychus: controversial theologian (A.D. 378–454)

Exotics: foreign plants

Fagged: tired

Fain: willingly

Familiar: demon in disguise (usually as a cat) which aids and abets a witch

Fare: food

Fillip: mere trifle

Flag: flagstone floor

Freaks: mischievous behaviour

Frieze: coarse woollen cloth

Front: forehead

Funchal: capital of Madeira

Fustian: turgid writing

Gall and wormwood: bitterness and rancour

Game covers: specially protected areas for game such as pheasant and grouse

Ganges: major Indian river

Girdled: surrounded

Gloaming: twilight

Gossamer: light and flimsy material which a spider's web is made of

Greatheart and Apollyon: two characters in Bunyan's *Pilgrim's Progress*: Greatheart is Christian's guide to the Celestial City; Apollyon is the Devil

Gripe: pain

Habergeon: coat of mail

Hebdomadal: weekly

Hebrew Ark: wooden chest saved from the

Great Flood by Noah and containing all the Jewish laws

Hercules: Greek hero of great strength and virility destroyed by Deianira who poisoned him with a shirt steeped in deadly venom

Hierophyte: initiating strings

High lows: a sort of ankle boot

'Him of Macedonia': Alexander the Great

Hindustani: Hindu language

Hoary lea: withered grass land

Holland pinafores: pinafores made of unbleached material

Holm: flat ground by river

Hose: stockings

Houri: beautiful women: in Islamic myths, the nymphs of Paradise

Huge city: London, probably

Humbug: hypocrisy

Ignis fatuus: misleading sign or light; ridiculous passion

Inanition: emptiness, starvation

Incubi: nightmarish things

Indian Messalina: Messalina was the notorious, lascivious wife of the Roman Emperor Claudius, and her name has become a byword for sexual incontinency. Catherine the Second of Russia was known as the Modern Messalina on account of her philandering

'ing': meadow

Interlocutrice: conversationalist

Irids: irises

Job's Leviathan: the Book of Job in the Old Testament tells the story of Job's patient suffering under tribulations. His Leviathan was a monster, possibly a whale or a crocodile, and certainly a symbol of the Devil

Jubilee: celebration

Juggernaut: mighty wagon used in Hindu ceremonies

King Ahasuerus: biblical character also known as the Emperor Xerxes and, in another context, the name can refer to a wandering Jew

Knoll: small hill

Lady clock: ladybird

Lappets: shawl or streamer from a woman's hat

Latmos: Mount Latmos in Greece, where Endymion, King of Elis, met Selene, the Moon Goddess. The myth was made famous by Keats's poem *Endymion*, published in 1818

Leads: roofs

Lendings: borrowed clothes

Letter-press: text to illustrations

Lexicon: dictionary

Ligature: binding material, like cord

Lilliput and Brobdingnag: from *Gulliver's Travels*, by Jonathan Swift. Lilliputians were a race of tiny people and Brobdingnagians a race of enormous people

Lineaments: features

Lozenged panes: diamond-shaped windowpanes

Lucre: money

Lustre: chandelier

Mahomet and the Mountain: the prophet Mahomet, or Mohammed, was the founder of the Muslim faith and lived from A.D. 560 to 632. The story of Mahomet and the mountain is based on one of the many thousand sayings about the man

Make shift: hurry up; manage to

Mandate: command

Manna: heavenly food which sustained the Israelites during their travels

Mark: design

Mediatrix: go-between (female)

Medusa: one of the three Gorgons of Greek mythology with snakes for hair

Meet: fitting

Men in green: sprites, elves or even the Irish leprechauns

Merino: very soft cloth made of pure wool or cashmere

Mien: bearing, expression

Millcote, in —shire: we learn that Millcote is 70 miles from London on the banks of the A—, and that the county was chiefly concerned with manufacturing interests. Thus it is fair to assume that Charlotte Brontë was referring to War-wickshire, and the river was the Avon

Modes: fashion

Moiety: half

Moreen: stout woollen or cotton material

Mother Bunches: Elizabethan landlady of an inn, famous in her time and whose reputation fostered many anecdotes. Even books were written about her, for example: 'Mother Bunches Closet Newly Broke Open' which contained salient advice for young men and women hoping to get married

Nebuchadnezzar: king of Babylon who in the Old Testament inflicted much suf-fering upon the people of Jerusalem

Nectar and ambrosia: food of the gods

Neophyte: novice, new convert

Niggard: mean person

'Noan faal': possibly 'not a fool' in dialect

North Midland shire: possibly Derbyshire

Novitiate: early training

Old gentleman: the Devil

''onding on snaw': looking like snow

Opera inamorata: hateful 'hired woman', i.e. mistress or prostitute

Orb: sphere

Organ of Adhesiveness: natural tendency to become attached

Organ of veneration: memory

Ostler: stableman at an inn

Ottoman: cushioned seat without a back or arms

Palmistry: telling fortunes by examining people's palms and tracing the lines on them

Palsy: paralysis

Parian mantle piece: The island of Paros in Greece was famed for its marble

Parley: talk

Parson in the pip: depressed parson

Parterre: allotment

Pastille: paste burnt as a fumigator

Paul and Silas's prison: St Paul and his fol-lower, Silas, were imprisoned in Mace-donia but managed to escape when, after singing praises to the Lord, a mighty earthquake destroyed the prison

Pauper: poor person

Paynim features: face of a Muslim

Paysannes: French peasants

Pelisse: cloak or mantle

Pendent: hanging

Philter: love potion

Phylactery: Hebrew box containing laws and texts

Pinch of snuff: powdered tobacco sniffed and inhaled as a stimulant or sometimes a sedative

Plainwork woman: woman who can do very simple and straightforward sewing jobs

Plate: silver- or gold-plated cutlery, plates, ornaments, etc

Plucked: failed in an exam

Poltroon: coward

Poor House: state-run workhouse where poor and destitute people were sent and in return for their labour had food and shelter, however meagre

Port: bearing

Porter: beer

Portmanteau: trunk for clothes

Possessed of a competency: having enough to live on

Post-chaise: carriage

Prominences which are said to indicate that

faculty: refers to the study of the bumps on people's heads which were said to determine their character and behaviour

Prospect: view

Quakerlike: the Quakers were, and still are, a fundamental Protestant sect

Quiz: odd, even ridiculous person

Rasselas: a moralistic novel with an Oriental setting, written by Samuel Johnson in 1759

Redd up: restored

Rent roll: register of lands owned and tenanted

Resurgam: I shall rise again

Rill: stream

Rizzio, Mary, David, Bothwell, and James Hepburn: Mary was Mary Queen of Scots; David Rizzio, her Italian secretary, was suspected of having an adulterous relationship with Mary and was thus murdered by her first husband, Lord Darnley, who was in turn murdered by James Hepburn, Earl of Bothwell. Bothwell became her second husband in 1567

Roagout: highly seasoned stew

Rubicon: point of no return

Rubric: direction for the conduct of Divine Service

Rush light: candle made from burning a slender rush

Ruth: pity

Salamander: legendary lizard-like creature thought to be able to live in fire

Samson: biblical hero who, like Hercules, possessed great strength, but who was also destroyed by a woman, Delilah; she cut off his hair and thus unmanned and blinded him

Saturnine: gloomy

Saul and David: Saul was King of the Israelites and the young David, who succeeded him as king, was able to calm the older man and subdue his anger by playing his harp

Seminary: school

Seraglio: sultan's palace, especially the part where women were kept

Seraph: celestial being

Shambles: butcher's slaughter-house

Sharpers: cheats, swindlers

Skirts: boundaries

Solomon: the biblical King Solomon, King of the Israelites

Sotto voce: quietly

Sovereign hand: God

Sparks: young men about town

Sphynx: Egyptian statue with the face of a woman and the body of a lion. In ancient myths, the sphynxes posed insuperable puzzles, and thus the Sphynx has come to be the embodiment of mystery

Spoony: sentimental lover

Stark: stiff, rigid

Stocks: wooden frame with holes for hands and feet into which criminals were publicly imprisoned usually for minor crimes

Suttee: Hindu widow who commits suicide by throwing herself upon her husband's funeral pyre

Swaths: ridges of cut grass

Switch: springy cane

Sybil: legendary prophetess and pronouncer of oracles

Sylph: spirit of the air

Tabernacle: mystical and venerated object

Take the veil: become a nun

Talisman: charm

Thrall: enslavement

Three-tailed bashaw: Turkish military commander or governor

Tinkler: tinker: wandering repairman of kettles and pans

Tonnage and Poundage: Customs duties imposed by Charles I unconstitutionally upon wine and other merchandise

Tricked out: dressed up

Tropes: descriptive use of words

Tucker: piece of lace or linen covering neck or shoulders

Turkey carpet: carpet from Turkey

Turnpike house: a staging-post where toll was collected

Tyne: loose

Typhus: dangerous fever, which is contagious

Tyrian dyed curtain: Tyre in Lebanon was famous at this time for cottons. Tyrian means purple

Upas-tree: Javanese tree with fatally poisonous sap

Vampyre: Germanic mythical ghost which leaves its grave after sundown and feeds from the blood of living beings

Vassalage: servants

Verdure: green vegetation

Vicinage: vicinity

Vignettes: engraved illustrations

Vinaigrettes: bottles or small boxes for holding aromatic and reviving vinegar

Virgil: Roman poet, died 19 B.C.

Visage: face

Vitals: essential being, nerve centre of one's body

Volatile salts: smelling salts used for reviving purposes

Vulcan: the Roman god of fire and patron of metal workers and blacksmiths

Wave girt: surrounded by sea

Wax: become

Welkin: sky

Wicket: small gate alongside a larger one

Widow's cap: the black cap traditionally worn by widows in mourning, sometimes years after the death of their husband

Wolfe, the death of: James Wolfe (1727–59) was the famous general who commanded the British forces at the siege of Quebec, at which he was killed. A very popular British hero

Wrest: pull

Glossary: Words and Phrases in French

Ami: friend

Badinage: banter

Beauté mâle: an ugliness which has a certain beauty

Bon soir: good evening

C'est là, ma gouvernante?: Is that my governess?

Carte blanche: full permission

Chez maman ... comme cela on apprend: at Mother's house, when lots of people were there, I used to follow them everywhere into the drawing-room and into their bedrooms: often I would watch the maids arrange their hair and dress them – and it was such good fun. You learn like that

Chiffonières: movable low cupboards

Choler: anger

Consoles: bookcases

Conte de fées: stories about fairies

Croquant: munching

Diablerie: devilish business

Du reste, il n'y avait pas de fées, et quand même il y en avait ...: anyway, there are no such things as fairies, and even if there were ...

Elles changent de toilettes: they are getting ready

En masse: together

En règle: to the rule

Équipages: crew/team

Est-ce que je ne puis pas prendre une seule de ces fleurs magnifiques, mademoiselle? Seulement pour compléter ma toilette: could I not just take one of these lovely flowers, Miss, to put the finishing touches to my outfit?

Est-ce que ma robe va bien? et mes souliers? et mes bras? Tenez, je crois que je vais danser: is my dress alright? and my shoes? and my arms? Wait, I think I shall dance

Et alors quel dommage: well, what a shame

Et cela droit signifier ... car c'est vrai, n'est ce pas Mademoiselle?: and that must mean that there's a present for me in there, and perhaps for you, too, Miss. Mr Rochester has spoken about you. He has asked me the name of my governess and whether she wasn't rather small, thin and a bit pale. I replied that you were, because it's true, isn't it, Miss?

Être: to be

Faux air: disguise

Gardez-vous bien: look after yourself carefully

Girandoles: branched candles

Il faut que je l'essaie et à l'instant même: I must try it immediately

J'y tiens: I have it

Jeune encore: young, as well

La belle passion: the great love affair

La Ligue des Rats, fable de La Fontaine: the League of Rats, a fable written by the famous French fabulist, Jean de La Fontaine (1621–95), who, through his fables about animals, managed to convey a great deal about human behaviour

Le cas: the thing to do

Ma boîte: my box

Mais oui mademoiselle: voilà cinq ou six heures que nous n'avons pas mangé: but yes, Miss: it must be five or six hours since we last ate

Mais oui, certainement: Yes, of course

Mesdames, vous êtes servies! ... J'ai bien faim, moi!: Ladies, dinner is served! ... I am very hungry!

Minois chiffonné: crumpled little face

Mon ange: my angel

Monsieur, je vous remercie mille fois de votre bonté. C'est comme cela maman faisait, n'est ce pas, monsieur?: Sir, I thank you a thousand times for your generosity. This is how Mother used to dance, isn't it?

N'est ce pas, monsieur, qu'il y a un cadeau pour Mademoiselle Eyre dans votre petit coffre?: There's a present for Miss Eyre in your little trunk, isn't there sir

Oh qu'elle y sera mal – peu confortable: oh it will be awful for her – so uncomfortable.

Par parenthèse: by the by

Parterre: flower-bed

Père noble de théâtre: grand old man of the theatre

Petit coffre: little trunk

Pour me donner une contenance: to give the impression of being composed

Prénomens: Christian names

Prête à croquer sa petite maman anglaise: ready to eat her little English mother

Qu'avez-vous donc? lui dit un de ces rats; parlez: What is wrong? one of the rats said to him; speak

Qu'avez-vous, mademoiselle? Vos doigts tremblent comme la feuille et vos joues sont rouges: mais rouges comme des cerises!: what is wrong, Miss? Your fingers are trembling like a leaf, and your cheeks are red: why, red as cherries!

Religieuses: nuns

Revenez bientôt, ma bonne amie, ma chère Mlle Jeannette: come back soon, my good friend, my dear Miss Jane

Sacques: loose gown falling from the shoulder to the floor like a train

Sans mademoiselle: without Miss

Surtout: overcoat

Taille d'athlète: athlete's physique

Tant pis: too bad

Tête-à-tête: solely in the company of

Tiens-tu tranquille, enfant, comprends-tu? Oh ciel! Que c'est beau: Keep calm, child, understand? Oh Heavens!, it's beautiful

Un vrai menteur: a real liar

Voiture: coach/carriage

Glossary: Words and Phrases in German

Bäuerinnen: German peasant women

'*Da trat hervor Einer, anzusehen wie die Sternen Nacht*': 'there trod one from thence who looked at the night stars' – quote from Schiller

German Gräfinnen: German baronesses

'*Ich erwäge die Gedanken in der Schale meines Zornes und die Werke mit dem Gewichte meines Grimms*': 'I weigh my thoughts in the scales of my sorrow and my acts in the weighing of my anger' – quote from the nineteenth-century German poet Schiller

Examination Questions

1. Read the following passage, and answer all the questions printed beneath it:

A passion of resentment fomented now within me.

Mrs Reed looked up from her work; her eye settled on mine, her fingers at the same time suspended their nimble movements.

'Go out of the room; return to the nursery,' was her mandate. My look or something else must have struck her as offensive, for she spoke with extreme though suppressed irritation. I got up, I went to the door; I came back again; I walked to the window, across the room, then close up to her.

Speak I must: I had been trodden on severely, and *must* turn: but how? What strength had I to dart retaliation at my antagonist? I gathered my energies and launched then in this blunt sentence –

'I am not deceitful: if I were, I should say I loved *you*; but I declare I do not love you: I dislike you the worst of anybody in the world except John Reed; and this book about the liar, you may give to your girl, Georgiana, for it is she who tells lies, and not I.'

Mrs Reed's hands still lay on her work inactive: her eye of ice continued to dwell freezingly on mine.

'What more have you to say?' she asked, rather in the tone in which a person might address an opponent of adult age than such as is ordinarily used to a child.

That eye of hers, that voice stirred every antipathy I had. Shaking from head to foot, thrilled with ungovernable excitement, I continued –

'I am glad you are no relation of mine: I will never call you aunt again so long as I live. I will never come to see you when I am grown up; and if any one asks me how I liked you, and how you treated me, I will say the very thought of you makes me sick, and that you treated me with miserable cruelty.'

(i) What provoked this outburst from Jane?

(ii) *I will never ... grown up* (lines 23–25). How did she, in fact, behave towards Mrs Reed after Robert Leaven came to Thornfield and told her of Mrs Reed's illness?

(iii) Show how vividly the character of Mrs Reed's hostility to Jane is conveyed in this passage.

(iv) By referring in detail to the passage, show how it conveys Jane's *passion of resentment* (line 1).

(*Oxford Local Examinations*)

2. Read the following passage, and answer all the questions printed beneath it:

And oh! where meantime was the hapless owner of this wreck? In what land? Under what auspices? My eye involuntarily wandered to the grey church tower near the gates, and I asked, 'Is he with Damer de Rochester, sharing the shelter of his narrow marble house?'

Some answer must be had to these questions. I could find it nowhere but at the inn, and thither, ere long, I returned. The host himself brought my breakfast into the parlour. I requested him to shut the door and sit down: I had some questions to ask him. But when he complied, I scarcely knew how to begin; such horror had I of the possible answers. And yet the spectacle of desolation I had just left prepared me in a measure for a tale of misery. The host was a respectable-looking, middle-aged man.

'You know Thornfield Hall, of course?' I managed to say at last.

'Yes, ma'am; I lived there once.'

'Did you?' Not in my time, I thought: you are a stranger to me.

'I was the late Mr Rochester's butler,' he added.

The late! I seemed to have received, with full force, the blow I had been trying to evade.

'The late!' I gasped. 'Is he dead?'

'I mean the present gentleman, Mr Edward's father,' he explained. I breathed again: my blood resumed its flow. Fully assured by these words that Mr Edward – *my* Mr Rochester (God bless him, wherever

he was!) – was at least alive: was, in short, 'the present gentleman.'
Gladdening words! It seemed I could hear all that was to come –
whatever the disclosures might be – with comparative tranquillity.
Since he was not in the grave, I could bear, I thought, to learn that
he was at the Antipodes.

(i) Describe the *wreck* (line 1) that Jane was looking at. What message
had brought her to the place?

(ii) Explain *his narrow marble house* (line 4).

(iii) Where and in what state did Jane find Edward Rochester?

(iv) Show how in this extract Charlotte Brontë conveys Jane's
anxiety and relief.

When the wedding was forbidden and she had heard the story of
Rochester's first marriage, what considerations made it difficult for
Jane to decide what to do? What hardships did she suffer before she
was received at Moor House?

Jane said 'Nature must be gladsome when I was so happy'. Show
how throughout the novel Charlotte Brontë makes nature sympathize
with Jane's fortunes, sad as well as happy.

(*Oxford Local Examinations*)

FOR THE BEST IN PAPERBACKS, LOOK FOR THE

PENGUIN PASSNOTES

This comprehensive series, designed to help O-level and CSE students, includes:

SUBJECTS
Biology
Chemistry
Economics
English Language
French
Geography
Human Biology
Mathematics
Modern Mathematics
Modern World History
Narrative Poems
Physics

SHAKESPEARE
As You Like It
Henry IV, Part I
Henry V
Julius Caesar
Macbeth
The Merchant of Venice
A Midsummer Night's Dream
Romeo and Juliet
Twelfth Night

LITERATURE
Arms and the Man
Cider With Rosie
Great Expectations
Jane Eyre
Kes
Lord of the Flies
A Man for All Seasons
The Mayor of Casterbridge
My Family and Other Animals
Pride and Prejudice
The Prologue to The Canterbury
    Tales
Pygmalion
Saint Joan
She Stoops to Conquer
Silas Marner
To Kill a Mockingbird
War of the Worlds
The Woman in White
Wuthering Heights

PENGUIN CLASSICS

THE LIBRARY OF EVERY CIVILIZED PERSON

Matthew Arnold	Selected Prose
Jane Austen	Emma
	Lady Susan, The Watsons, Sanditon
	Mansfield Park
	Northanger Abbey
	Persuasion
	Pride and Prejudice
	Sense and Sensibility
Anne Brontë	The Tenant of Wildfell Hall
Charlotte Brontë	Jane Eyre
	Shirley
	Villette
Emily Brontë	Wuthering Heights
Samuel Butler	Erewhon
	The Way of All Flesh
Thomas Carlyle	Selected Writings
Wilkie Collins	The Moonstone
	The Woman in White
Charles Darwin	The Origin of the Species
Charles Dickens	American Notes for General Circulation
	Barnaby Rudge
	Bleak House
	The Christmas Books
	David Copperfield
	Dombey and Son
	Great Expectations
	Hard Times
	Little Dorrit
	Martin Chuzzlewit
	The Mystery of Edwin Drood
	Nicholas Nickleby
	The Old Curiosity Shop
	Oliver Twist
	Our Mutual Friend
	The Pickwick Papers
	Selected Short Fiction
	A Tale of Two Cities

PENGUIN CLASSICS

THE LIBRARY OF EVERY CIVILIZED PERSON

Arnold Bennett	**The Old Wives' Tale**
Joseph Conrad	**Heart of Darkness**
	Nostromo
	The Secret Agent
	The Shadow-Line
	Under Western Eyes
E. M. Forster	**Howard's End**
	A Passage to India
	A Room With a View
	Where Angels Fear to Tread
Thomas Hardy	**The Distracted Preacher and Other Tales**
	Far From the Madding Crowd
	Jude the Obscure
	The Mayor of Casterbridge
	The Return of the Native
	Tess of the d'Urbervilles
	The Trumpet Major
	Under the Greenwood Tree
	The Woodlanders
Henry James	**The Aspern Papers and The Turn of the Screw**
	The Bostonians
	Daisy Miller
	The Europeans
	The Golden Bowl
	An International Episode and Other Stories
	Portrait of a Lady
	Roderick Hudson
	Washington Square
	What Maisie Knew
	The Wings of the Dove
D. H. Lawrence	**The Complete Short Novels**
	The Plumed Serpent
	The Rainbow
	Selected Short Stories
	Sons and Lovers
	The White Peacock
	Women in Love